Advanced Academic Writing

An Illustrated Program

Volume One: The Four Basic Elements

Teacher Manual
with CD of Actual Research Paper Comments

Michael Clay Thompson

Royal Fireworks Press
Unionville, New York

Roble 1

Barney Roble

Ms. DeMeener

English Honors

25 April 2008

The Noble Character of Alexander

The literature about Alexander the Great is ex
Writers ancient and modern have probed the availa
of his life in search of the factors that enable
to accomplish seemingly impossible feats of mili
One potential cause of his extraordinary succes
One potential cause of his character. St
...and magnanimity of his character.

Rob

Works Cited

Cartledge, Paul. Alexander the Great. New York: Overlook,
2004.

Cummings, Lewis V. Alexander the Great. New York

Royal Fireworks Press
First Avenue, PO Box 399
Unionville, NY 10988-0399
(845) 726-4444
FAX: (845) 726-3824
email: mail@rfwp.com
website: rfwp.com
ISBN:
Student Book: 978-0-88092-674-4
Teacher Book: 978-0-88092-675-1

Printed and bound in the United States of America using vegetable-based inks on acid-free recycled paper and environmentally-friendly cover coatings by the Royal Fireworks Printing Co. of Unionville, New York.

Design and text by Michael Clay Thompson

Table of Contents

Att 1

Larry Att
Mr. Rheus
English Honors
25 April 2008

The Noble Character of Alexander

The literature about Alexander the Great is extensive. Writers ancient and modern have probed the available facts of his life in search of the factors that enabled Alexander ...lish seemingly impossible feats of military genius. ... might be the

Matticle 1

Graham Matticle

Ms. Eltoh

English Honors

25 April 2008

The Noble Character of Alexander

The literature about Alexander the Great is extensive. Writers ancient and modern have probed the available facts of his life in search of the factors that enabled Alexander to accomplish seemingly impossible feats of military genius. One potential cause of his extraordinary success might be the nobility and magnanimity of his character. Stories abound about Alexander's respect for local cultures and for the bravery of his enemies. He often often absorbed defeated leaders into his own army, appointing them to high and responsible rank. When after defeating Darius, he gave chase and finally found the dead king alone and unattended, Alexander covered Darius with his own cloak:

> He gazed for a moment at the poor corpse that alone was the spoil of the long race, then took off his cloak and wrapped it around the body of his predecessor . . . (Cummings 258)

Alexander's respect for Darius

Here is an MLA page in progress. Look how the long quotation is indented ten spaces.

Ask students why there is an ellipsis (...) at the end of the long quotation.

These blue boxes appear only in the Teacher Manual.

Matticle 4

Works Cited

Cartledge, Paul. Alexander the Great. New York: Overlook, 2004.

Cummings, Lewis V. Alexander the Great. New York: Grove, 1968.

Fox, Robin Lane. Alexander the Great. New York: Penguin, 2004.

Green, Peter. Alexa nder of Macedon, 356-323 B.C.: A Historical Biography. Berkeley: U of California P, 1991.

Check date

1. You Begin with a Decision.

A Great Opportunity

If you want to go to college, have a professional career, and live life with an educated mind, then you can do all of these things; you must simply make a strong decision. The decision is whether or not you will learn to write formal academic English. Actually, the decision is unavoidable; if you decide not to think about it, it will be the same as deciding not to.

If you accept this challenge, it will be a courageous undertaking. It will take years of mature commitment and self-discipline as your ability gets stronger. You will master complex elements of language and finally combine them into a single, unified talent.

Be very realistic: think about all of the formal essays, exams, critical discussions, and research papers you will be assigned in high school, college, and graduate school. You will receive these academic writing assignments not only in English courses, but in *every course*—in all of your science, history, and other courses as well. Add to that the reports, reviews, and statements you will have to make in your profession throughout your lifetime.

What these assignments have in common, without exception, is that *you have to write them.* If you write badly, you will write them all badly. The risks for your grades are clear. If, on the other hand, you write well, then your assignments will be well-written, and the benefits of that are also clear.

Who has the right to say that anyone's writing is bad? Is it not rude to call any writing *bad*? Without question, we live in a democracy, and each of us is free to write as we choose, but with so much at stake, we must not be distracted from the unsentimental truth: in education and the professions, there *are* formal academic writing rules and standards, and your teachers, professors, and professional colleagues *will* require you to adhere to them. In your private diary, you can have grammar errors and eccentric writing mannerisms, but in the academic world, and in the professional world that expects academic standards, it is not up to you; you will be expected to apply formal, standard, academic writing rules, and as you work on all of your written assignments, you either will know what you are doing—or not.

The Right Decision

If you have turned the page, and you are still reading this book, then you realize you will have to know how to write advanced academic English. You do not want to be unprepared for excellence. You know that you need tough writing assignments that will help you learn.

The good news is that your decision to learn advanced academic writing puts you on a path that is not only necessary but exciting. First, learning about language is exciting. In the process you acquire a powerful academic vocabulary; a grammatical understanding of the logic of correct, clear, and meaningful sentences; and a sense of formal essay structure that lets you organize your thoughts so that your reader can understand you. The purpose of formal academic writing is to communicate clearly, saying exactly what you really mean and think. Second, each of these studies (vocabulary, grammar, essay structure) changes your life, leaving you comfortable and confident and giving you a deep enjoyment of the beauty, integrity, and truth of language. It is fun to know what you are doing.

A Different Kind of Book: An Assignment Book

This book is not a traditional textbook. It is also not a reference book. It is what we might call an **assignment book**. Part of what that means is that this book does not provide all of the knowledge necessary to complete its writing assignments; if it did, it would have to be two thousand pages long. For example, this is not a vocabulary book that will teach you the academic words you will need to use in your writing. You will find strong academic vocabulary in *The Word Within the Word, Volume One*. This is also not a grammar textbook, even though correct grammar will be a key element of the correct writing in these assignments. You will find elaborate grammar instruction in *The Magic Lens, Volume One*.

Forty Writing Focus Points

What this book does give you is four advanced academic writing assignments, with special **points of focus** in each assignment. These focus points accumulate throughout the book, and continue to accumulate in Volumes Two and Three. In Volume One there are forty of these special points, in Volume Two forty more, and in volume three forty more. These special focus points are the result of decades of grading advanced formal research papers; they are the very areas shown to give students the most difficulty.

The Basic Expectations of All Four Writing Assignments: an Overview

Research Papers: You Write About What You Have Read in Books

This is serious, grown-up work; you are beginning a path that will lead to professional, publishable writing. That fact demands a no-kid-stuff tone of maturity for everything we will do. None of these four papers will be loose opinion pieces, or emotional expressions of personal insight. They will be short but precise research papers that require you to use quotations from books to support your conclusions about actual knowledge. You will have to read and think before writing, and then include documented long and short quotations to make your case, showing that your conclusion is not merely a matter of your unsupported opinion but the truth, as supported by facts and expert statement.

In other words, these papers cannot be written off the top of your head; they are to be about academic topics. You must choose subjects that you do not already know about and that have serious academic content. Likewise, you may use only serious academic sources for your quotations. Elementary encyclopedias are not allowed. You are not allowed to reuse a topic that you wrote about last year. You have to learn about the topic before you can write about it.

MLA Method

There are several standards for formal research papers, but the most widely used method in high schools and colleges is the Modern Language Association or MLA method. The Modern Language Association publishes the *MLA Handbook*, which contains the complete collection of MLA standards. That is the method we support and that we require in this program. In advanced academic writing, we always adhere *exactly* to whatever method we use; the expectation is that all formatting rules will be followed to the letter.

Short Length, High Standards

The emphasis in these assignments is quality, not quantity. At this stage of your learning, there is no reason for you to write ten-page or twenty-page papers; you will face most of your challenges in a three-page paper. By keeping your papers short, we can focus our attention on quality, insisting that the English, the essay structure, and the format of the papers be as perfect as possible. You will have time to focus on each detail. In formal academic writing, little details are big deals.

Formal, Standard English

Although we will discuss details of style at length later, we can say that your papers are to be written in standard academic English. They must contain no grammar or punctuation errors. You may not use contractions (*don't*, *didn't*) in your own sentences, though they may appear in quotations. You may not use first person (*I think*, *in my opinion*) or refer to yourself or your paper (*In this paper, on the following page*) in any way. You may not use groovy spellings such as *lite* or *thru*. You must use academic vocabulary (*individual*, not *guy*; *impressive*, not *cool; excellent*, not *awesome*) and avoid all clichés, which are worn-out, stock expressions such as *the bottom line is*, *at the end of the day*, *as cold as ice*, *as clear as mud*, and so forth.

Not Handwritten

This is advanced work, and advanced work is not submitted in handwriting. You will be expected to type the paper yourself on a computer word-processor; preparing your own papers is a critical skill you will need. You will type the paper in Courier type font, which is one of the standard type fonts on computers. Courier is the font used in the sample illustrations, as you see below. A paper done in a different font will be returned to be redone. The paper will be double-spaced.

Integrity: No Plagiarism

The sentences in your papers must be entirely your own work unless you document otherwise. All quotation and even paraphrasing (putting someone's ideas in your own words) from a book or article must be clearly documented. Copying someone else's work is called *plagiarism*, and it **will result in a grade of zero**. The MLA method provides a simple, alphabetized Works Cited method for citing—documenting—other writers' work, either their words or their ideas. We will look at the Works Cited instructions in detail later. The main point is that you always—at all times—distinguish honestly and clearly between your own words or ideas and someone else's words or ideas.

Thompson 4

Works Cited

Cartledge, Paul. Alexander the Great. New York: Overlook, 2004.

Cummings, Lewis V. Alexander the Great. NewYork: Grove, 1968.

Fox, Robin Lane. Alexander the Great. New York: Penguin, 2004.

Green, Peter. Alexander, of Macedon, 356-323 B.C.: A Historical Biography. Berkeley: U of California P, 1991.

Rigorous Grading

Your teacher knows you best and will make the final decisions about the grading method that he or she will use, but I will speak to you as though you were in my own classroom; that way, even if your teacher is more forgiving than I would be, you will learn what to expect from many teachers and professors in the future. If I were grading your papers, they would be rigorously graded. I always expect the errors you make to be at least at grade level; if you turn in papers filled with elementary errors of spelling and punctuation that you were supposed to have mastered in earlier grades, you cannot receive a passing grade. If education is going to work, we cannot continue reteaching the same knowledge year after year; you have to master the content and advance. Anyone might make an occasional elementary mistake or two, but if there is a pattern of negligent carelessness, if you have multiple spelling errors and punctuation errors per page, then that is not passing work. Advanced academic writing contains no careless elementary mistakes, and strict grading now can teach you that standard.

Standard (Real) Proofreader's Marks

Just as there are standard rules for grammar, spelling, and punctuation, there are also standard marks of correction, called *proofreader's marks*, that the educational and publishing professions use to mark writing errors. In Volume One we will emphasize ten standard ways of marking errors (adding more marks with volume two and three of the program) that the professional world uses. Some proofreader's marks that we will feature in this book are:

1.	Delete	`I have my very own example.`
2.	Insert period	`Clouds approached It rained.`
3.	Insert comma	`He was strict, stern and serious.`
4.	Insert space	`Alexander reactedquickly.` #
5.	Close up	`Suddenly, the bat tle began.`
6.	Start new paragraph	`It ended.` ¶ `The next day we departed.`
7.	Spell out or spelling error	`It was the 4th time that week.` sp
8.	Transpose (switch)	`It began to suddenly rain.`
9.	Awkward wording	`It went then higher as a thing gradual.` awk
10.	Subject/verb disagreement	`The reason for the errors are this.` s/v

Study these marks carefully. Your teacher will use these on your papers.

Three-part Essay Structure

We often introduce the essay structure to students by using a simple, five-paragraph model. In this five-paragraph learning model, there is a one-paragraph introduction, three paragraphs of body, and a one-paragraph conclusion. The short research papers we will write are essays with introductions, bodies, and conclusions, but our essays will be more advanced. Our essays will have more than five paragraphs. We might have multiple paragraphs in the introduction, seven paragraphs in the body, and more than one paragraph in the conclusion. Good essays reflect the structures of their subjects, and so the essay will have as many paragraphs as the subject needs. How does essay structure work? Study the graphic on the following page closely:

1. **The entire essay is about its thesis (its main idea)**. If we let *t* stand for thesis, we see in the diagram on the following page that the thesis is presented in the **introduction** (*t?*), that a sequence of evidence for the thesis is presented in the **body** (*t1, t2, t3*), and that the meaning of all this information for the thesis is explained in the **conclusion** (*t!*). (Note: A five-paragraph biographical article in an encyclopedia is not an essay because it does not have a three-part essay *structure*. If the first sentence is "Shakespeare was born on... and the last sentence is "Shakespeare died on...", then the passage is only a chronological list of facts, lacking a thesis, an introduction, and a conclusion. Do not use an encyclopedia article as your model.)

2. **The entire structure is precisely organized.** *Everything* is organized. The paragraphs of the body are in a logical order (*t1, t2, t3*), and within the paragraphs the sentences are in a logical order (*a, b, c, d*). Late paragraphs may depend upon facts presented in early paragraphs.

3. **The parts of the essay are connected (*c*), and their relationships to one another are clear at each connection**. Many essays fail at paragraph transitions because the reader cannot understand whether the new paragraph is a new idea or only a new example of the same idea. Special, connecting words (*c*) such as *on the other hand*, *in contrast*, or *furthermore* must be written at the seams when the connection is not clear. One good way to connect a paragraph to the paragraph before it is to use a D,I complex sentence beginning with a dependent clause. The dependent clause captures the point of the previous paragraph, and then the independent clause introduces the point of the present paragraph. If we have just explained that Jefferson sold his library, and are now going to discuss the improvements he made to his house, we might begin our new paragraph this way: *After Jefferson sold his library, he used the money to make improvements in Monticello.*

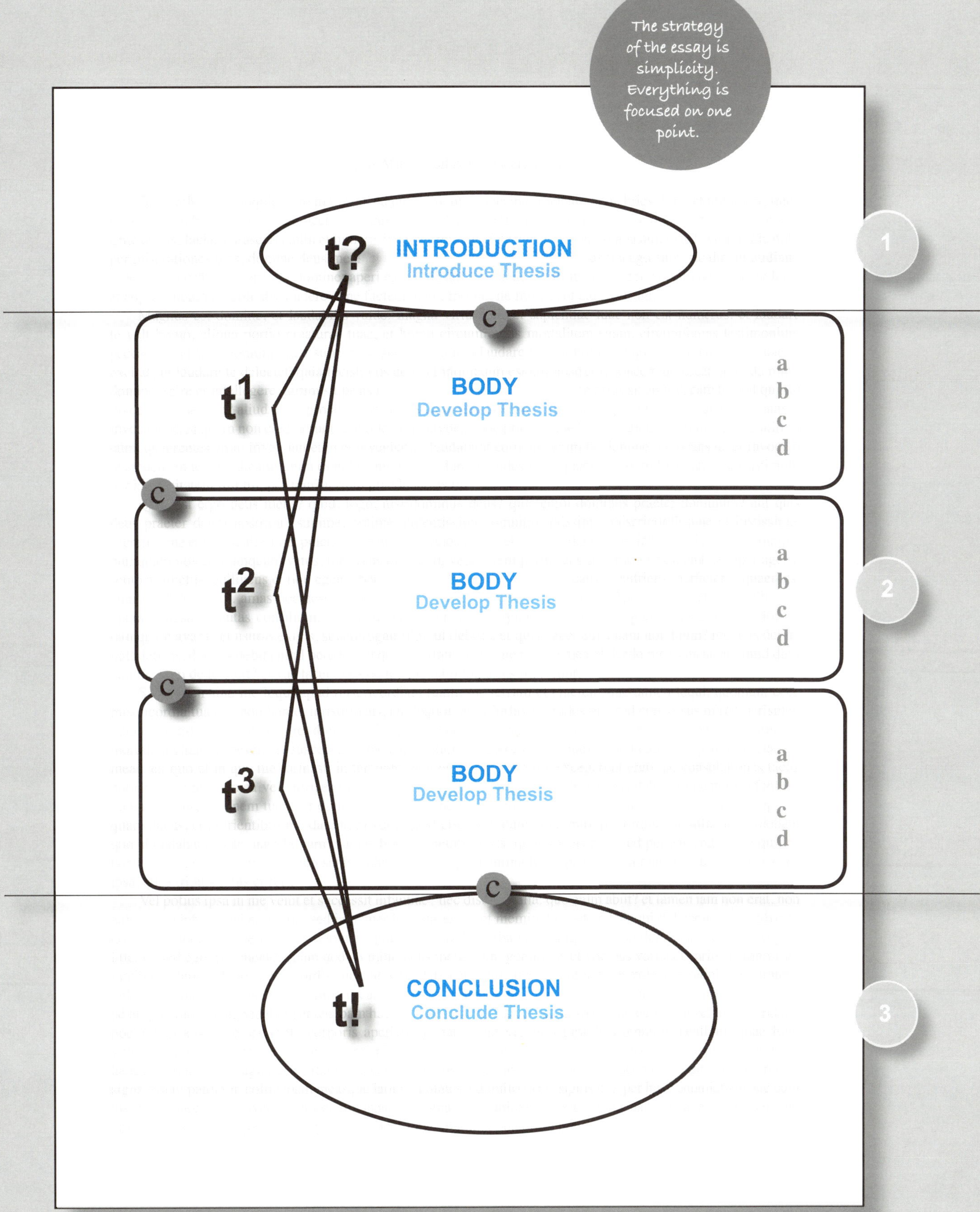
The strategy of the essay is simplicity. Everything is focused on one point.
t?
INTRODUCTION
Introduce Thesis
1
c
t1
BODY
Develop Thesis
a
b
c
d
c
t2
BODY
Develop Thesis
a
b
c
d
2
c
t3
BODY
Develop Thesis
a
b
c
d
c
t!
CONCLUSION
Conclude Thesis
3

2. The Basics of an MLA Paper

Clarity and Simplicity

Not long ago, writing a research paper was a frustrating and complex process. The Modern Language Association changed that with its MLA method which reinvented the process, making it vastly easier without sacrificing quality or clarity. For a full presentation of the MLA method, consult the *MLA Handbook*, but in this book we will focus on the central MLA standards:

1. **No title page**. An MLA paper does not have a separate title page. Instead, the required information is included at the top left margin of page one: student name, then teacher name, then course title, then date. The title of the paper follows and is exactly (not nearly) centered.

2. **Double-spacing**. An MLA paper is double-spaced, period. Some other methods single-space long quotations, or add extra blank lines at times, but in an MLA paper there are no such variations. Everything, even a long quotation, is double-spaced.

3. **One-inch margins**. An MLA paper uses one-inch margins on all four sides of each page. The exception is the header (the student name and page number), which is flush right and one-half inch down from the top of each page. The right margin of the paper should be **ragged right**, not **justified**. When we justify a page as in the small example at right, all of the lines line up on the right side; do not justify your paper because that destroys correct spacing between words.

4. **Parenthetical documentation and Works Cited**. At the end of an MLA paper, there is a list of every work you have cited, showing exactly where you found each quotation, paraphrase, or idea by someone else. These works are listed alphabetically by authors' last names. Each quotation in your paper is followed by the author's name and the page number of the book where the quotation appears. Look at the following page, and notice how the parenthetical notes connect to specific titles listed in the Works Cited. Notice how the period comes after the parentheses in a short quotation, but before it in a long quotation.

Let us look in more detail at the rules for quotation.

O'Dramah 1

HEADER

Mel O'Dramah

Ms. Tearius

English Honors

15 September 2008

The Magnanimous Mind of Alexander

RAGGED RIGHT

Writers ancient and modern have probed the facts of Alexander the Great's life in search of the factors that enabled him to accomplish seemingly impossible feats of military genius. One potential cause of his extraordinary success might be the nobility of his character. Stories abound about Alexander's respect for local cultures and for the bravery of his enemies. He often absorbed defeated leaders into his own army, appointing them to high rank.

At the battle of Gaugamela, Alexander's generals unanimously advised him to attack Darius's huge army at night when darkness would provide some advantage. "Alexander," he replied, "Does not steal his victories" (Fox 231). When, after defeating Darius, he gave chase and finally found the king's chariot, Alexander found the king dead, his body unattended:

> When Alexander reached it, the only cargo it carried was the dead body of Darius. He gazed for a moment at the poor corpse that alone was the spoil of the long race, then took off his cloak and wrapped it around the body of his predecessor. (Cummings 258)

Alexander's respect for opponents is also seen in his famous encounter with Diogenes of Sinope. Knowing Diogenes's

The names in the parentheticals and the names in the Works Cited are identical.

A name in a parenthetical MUST appear in the Works Cited page.

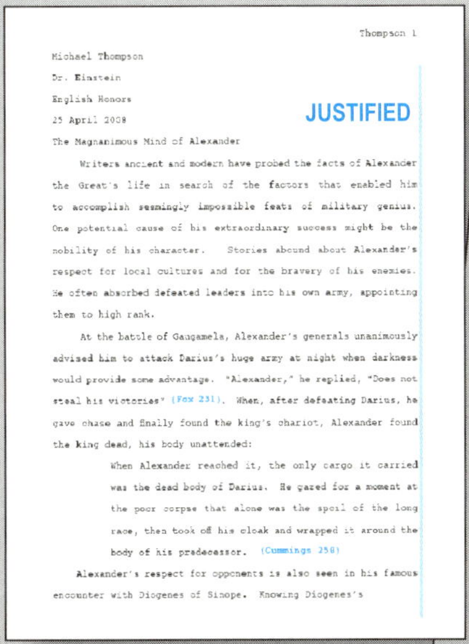

Thompson 1

Michael Thompson

Dr. Einstein

English Honors

25 April 2008

JUSTIFIED

The Magnanimous Mind of Alexander

Writers ancient and modern have probed the facts of Alexander the Great's life in search of the factors that enabled him to accomplish seemingly impossible feats of military genius. One potential cause of his extraordinary success might be the nobility of his character. Stories abound about Alexander's respect for local cultures and for the bravery of his enemies. He often absorbed defeated leaders into his own army, appointing them to high rank.

At the battle of Gaugamela, Alexander's generals unanimously advised him to attack Darius's huge army at night when darkness would provide some advantage. "Alexander," he replied, "Does not steal his victories" (Fox 231). When, after defeating Darius, he gave chase and finally found the king's chariot, Alexander found the king dead, his body unattended:

> When Alexander reached it, the only cargo it carried was the dead body of Darius. He gazed for a moment at the poor corpse that alone was the spoil of the long race, then took off his cloak and wrapped it around the body of his predecessor. (Cummings 258)

Alexander's respect for opponents is also seen in his famous encounter with Diogenes of Sinope. Knowing Diogenes's

O'Dramah 4

Works Cited

Cartledge, Paul. Alexander the Great. New York: Overlook, 2004.

Cummings, Lewis V. Alexander the Great. New York: Grove, 1968.

Fox, Robin Lane. Alexander the Great. New York: Penguin, 2004.

Green, Peter. Alexander of Macedon, 356-323 B.C.: A Historical Biography. Berkeley: U of California P, 1991.

Quotations, and the Great Integrity of Scholarship

A quotation is a passage in a book or other text that you put in your essay as evidence or example. When we show our reader a quote from another author, we are participating in a great tradition of honor and integrity, and scholars for centuries have taken pride in being meticulous about giving honest credit to the outstanding work of others. When you quote, you copy the exact words of the passage, and in your paper you place quotation marks around the quotation if it is short, or you indent it if it is a longer passage. Sometimes students think that a quotation means that they are looking for a passage that has *quotation marks in the book*; no, a quotation is any passage that you wish to show the reader of your paper. Not every passage in a book deserves to be quoted. The quotations in a research paper are like the special objects in a display case. They are special evidence that supports or illustrates our thesis.

Long quotations and Short Quotations

The MLA method treats long and short quotations differently:

> A **short quotation** (four lines or fewer) is enclosed in quotation marks, followed by one blank space, followed by a parenthetical documentation including the author's last name and page number (no comma between them), and the **period after the parenthetical**. *We* put the quotation marks to show exactly where the author's words begin and end.
>
> A **long quotation** (five lines or more) is not enclosed in quotation marks but is indented ten spaces—exactly ten, not nine or eleven—followed by two blank spaces and the parenthetical. Ordinary paragraphs are only indented five spaces. In a long quotation the period comes at the end of the quote, **before the parenthetical**.
>
> The **parenthetical documentation** (between parentheses) gives the author's last name, and the reader can turn to the **Works Cited** page at the end of the paper, where the authors are listed alphabetically, to learn more about the source of the quotation. You also put a parenthetical note if you are not quoting exact words but you are paraphrasing or just giving credit for an idea; see the Salvatore parenthetical on the following page.

There are three quotations in the sample page at right. Study each one carefully, noting each detail of the way it is presented and documented. Be sure to notice the spaces and the periods. For visual clarity, we will put the quotations and parentheticals in blue:

Burnetick 1

Cy Burnetick

Ms. O'Ffied

English 201

10 October 2007

PERIOD

The Indignation of William Lloyd Garrison

Frederick Douglass, the escaped slave who became an eloquent voice in the abolitionist movement, was exceptional not only for his intellectual genius that allowed him to educate himself but also for the indignation that he generated in others who heard his speeches. In his classic narrative, Douglass said:

> So profoundly ignorant of the nature of slavery are many persons, that they are stubbornly incredulous whenever they read or listen to any recital of the cruelties which are daily inflicted on its victims. They do not deny that slaves are held as property, but that terrible fact seems to convey to their minds no idea of injustice. (Douglass 40)

William Lloyd Garrison, the editor of the Liberator, said, after hearing Douglass speak, that he "never hated slavery so intensely as at that moment" (Johnston 234). Garrison was not alone in his admiration for Douglass, nor was he alone in his fervent indignation over the horrifying practice of slavery. When Garrison originally founded the Liberator, his anti-slavery publication, he solicited the support and opinion of a number of prominent individuals in Massachussetts (Salvatore 39). In The Age of Liberation, Susan Kare observes that Garrison's base of social support included important community figures who "provided both moral support and a considerable degree of financial support for the fledgling publication" (Kare 87).

This support is to some degree surprising because Garrison was viewed from the outset as among the most extreme and radical advocates of emancipation, and his denuciations of the evil of slavery reached a pitch

The MLA method lets you identify other writers' words perfectly.

Bartlett 4

Works Cited

Douglass, Frederick. The Narrative of My Life as a Slave. New York: Auden UP, 2004.

Johnston, Joseph. Observations on the War. Chicago: Harple, 2001.

Kare, Susasn. The Age of Liberation. New York: Randle, 1968.

Salvatore, Fredo. How William Lloyd Garrison and the Abolitionist Movement Raised Social Consciousness in the

More details about quotations.

When you quote words by someone else, you *must not misquote*. When you say someone else said something, he or she must have said it—exactly it. Your quotation, in other words, must be the perfect truth. You may not change a single word unless you follow two rules for such changes: (1) you use an **ellipsis** (. . .) to show an omission, or (2) **brackets** [like this] to show added or inserted words. You are not required to quote entire sentences; you may quote parts of sentences, so long as you do not omit words in a deceptive way that distorts meaning.

You should have a **balance** between your words and quotations. If your paper is almost entirely in your *own words*, it contains inadequate evidence. If the paper is just a long *series of quotations*, it seems like a book report. There must be a balance. Half to two-thirds of the paper should be in your own words; the quotations appear within the framework you write, like chips in a cookie. You will usually have an assortment of short and long quotations, and they should support your case without overwhelming the paper. A typical paper might have several short quotations and one long quotation per page. Do not fill an entire page or more with a gigantic quotation; it is rarely necessary to quote for more than six lines.

In most research papers the quotations come from **multiple sources**, proving that you have been thorough and that multiple experts agree with your thesis. (If you discover serious opinion contradicting your thesis, do not ignore it or conceal it; quote it too, and discuss the disagreement in your essay. The purpose of research is to find the truth, not to win an argument.) There are exceptions to the multiple-source rule, as when you interpret a classic novel, quoting exclusively from the novel.

It is important not to let quotations create **awkward breaks** in the flow of your essay. Write phrases that lead smoothly into quotations. Instead of clumsy, boring wordings such as "*The reader will see proof of this from the quotation that follows*," just use a content-based, graceful phrase such as "*Frederick Douglass replied that*," and then quote his words.

Study the two short quotations on the page at right; they are only pieces of sentences, selected to make a smooth flow possible. Notice, as mentioned above, that you do not have to quote entire sentences; you can choose where in a sentence to begin quoting, and this lets you construct graceful transitions from your words into the quotation.

Ehrinn 1

Marge Ehrin

Mr. Spellman

English 201

10 October 2007

The Indignation of William Lloyd Garrison

Frederick Douglass, the escaped slave who became an eloquent voice in the abolitionist movement, was exceptional not only for his intellectual genius that allowed him to educate himself but also for the indignation that he generated in others who heard his speeches. Douglass was a powerful communicator:

> So profoundly ignorant of the nature of slavery are many persons, that they are . . . incredulous whenever they read or listen to any recital of the cruelties which are daily inflicted on its victims. They do not deny that slaves are held as property, but that terrible fact seems to convey to their minds no idea of injustice. (Douglass 40)

William Lloyd Garrison, the editor of the Liberator, said, after hearing Douglass speak, that he "never hated slavery so intensely as [he did] at that moment" (Johnston 234). Garrison was not alone in his admiration for Douglass, nor was he alone in his fervent indignation over the horrifying practice of slavery. When Garrison originally founded the Liberator, his anti-slavery publication, he solicited the support and opinion of a number of prominent individuals in Massachussetts. In The Age of Liberation, Susan Kare observes that Garrison's base of social support included important community figures who "provided both moral support and a considerable degree of financial support for the fledgling publication" (Kare 87).

This support is to some degree surprising because Garrison was viewed from the outset as among the most extreme and radical advocates of emancipation, and his denuciations of the evil of slavery reached a pitch

All Quotations are Connected to the Works Cited Page

As we have already seen, one aspect of advanced writing that cannot be compromised is integrity. When we use other people's work, either their words or their ideas, we must indicate the true source of that work to the reader. We follow each quotation with a parenthetical note containing the author's last name and the page number of the book where we found the words. There is *no comma* between these two items:

`(Cummings 231)`

This lets the reader turn to the Works Cited page, scan down the alphabetized names to *Cummings*, and find the book, its title, city of publication, publisher, and date of publication.

Like the rest of the paper, the Works Cited page is double-spaced and has a one-inch margin all around, with the header one-half inch down at the top. The listings are flush left in their first lines, but indented five spaces afterwards—the opposite of the way we treat paragraphs. For now we will look at the simplest listing, a book by one author. The listing must be exact:

1. Author's last name.
2. Comma and one space.
3. Author's first name.
4. Period and two spaces.
5. Book title, underlined.
6. Period (not underlined), two spaces.
7. City of publication.
8. Colon and one space.
9. Publisher, abbreviated.
10. Comma, and one space.
11. Date of publication.
12. Period.

`Murphy, Mary.  The War in the Pacific.  Chicago: Bibliobooks, 2001.`

The *MLA Handbook* provides a long list of publisher abbreviations: *Random House* is just *Random*, *Penguin Books* is *Penguin*, *University of Chicago Press* is just *U of Chicago P*, and *Harvard University Press* is just *Harvard UP*. Notice in the Peter Green listing at right that there are no periods after the *U* or the *P*.

Notice that in Courier type font, which we are using for our papers, we use underlining instead of italics. Underline and italics are regarded as the same thing, but in Times Roman *italics looks good*, whereas in *Courier italics looks bad*, so we underline in Courier.

Thompson 4

Works Cited

Cartledge, Paul. Alexander the Great. New York: Overlook, 2004.

Cummings, Lewis V. Alexander the Great. New York: Grove, 1968.

Fox, Robin Lane. Alexander the Great. New York: Penguin, 2004.

Green, Peter. Alexander of Macedon, 356-323 B.C.: A Historical Biography. Berkeley: U of Californi

Rogers, Guy MacLean. Alexander: The Ambiguity of Gr New York: Random, 2004.

Work

Cartledge, Paul. Alexander the 2004.

Cummings, Lewis V. Alexander t 1968.

Fox, Robin Lane. Alexander the 2004.

Green, Peter. Alexander of Mac Historical Biography. Ber

Rogers, Guy MacLean. Alexander New York: Random, 2004.

The Works Cited page is expected to be perfect because it shows other people's work.

Thompson 4

Works Cited

Cartledge, Paul. Alexander the Great. New York: Overlook, 2004.

Cummings, Lewis V. Alexander the Great. New York: Grove, 1968.

Fox, Robin Lane. Alexander the Great. New York: Penguin, 2004.

Green, Peter. Alexander of Mace Historical Biography. Berk

Rogers, Guy MacLean. Alexander: New York: Random, 2004.

Thompson 4

Works Cited

Cartledge, Paul. Alexander the Great. New York: Overlook, 2004.

Cummings, Lewis V. Alexander the Great. New York: Grove, 1968.

Fox, Robin Lane. Alexander the Great. New York: Penguin, 2004.

Green, Peter. Alexander of Macedon, 356-323 B.C.: A Historical Biography. Berkeley: U of California P, 1991.

Rogers, Guy MacLean. Alexander: The Ambiguity of Greatness. New York: Random, 2004.

Thompson 4

Works Cited

Cartledge, Paul. Alexander the Great. New York: Overlook, 2004.

Cummings, Lewis V. Alexander the Great. New York: Grove, 1968.

Fox, Robin Lane. Alexander the Great. New York: Penguin, 2004.

Green, Peter. Alexander of Macedon, 356-323 B.C.: A Historical Biography. Berkeley: U of California P, 1991.

Rogers, Guy MacLean. Alexander: The Ambiguity of Greatness

Cartledge, Paul. Ale 2004.

Cummings, Lewis V. A 1968.

Fox, Robin Lane. Ale 2004.

Green, Peter. Alexan Historical Biog

A Sample Paper

Advanced academic writing, especially when it involves strict adherence to a standard method such as MLA, is a lot to learn. We could continue studying details for hundreds of pages, but that would become overwhelming; it would create more confusion than illumination. Sometimes the best way to learn something is to discuss the basics and then look at an example.

On the next three pages you will see a simple example of the advanced academic writing we will do. It is not a perfect paper, but it is a three-page MLA-style paper in which all of the quotations are taken from one book. This is the kind of paper you will write if you are analyzing a single work of literature, giving insight to an important element of the story or making a case for how the story should be interpreted.

This sample paper is about *Frankenstein*, by Mary Shelley. She was a brilliant woman, the daughter of the genius Mary Wollstonecraft and the wife of the great British poet Percy Shelley. Notice that the paper makes no attempt to summarize the entire plot; rather, the thesis focuses on one small but important element: the intelligence and humanity of the monster.

Because this is a literary think-piece, there is only one book in the Works Cited, and all of the quotes come from it. As a result, the parenthetical notations do not have to keep mentioning the author every time; after the first one, `(Shelley 106)`, the subsequent parentheticals can just use the page number in parentheses.

One of the most important things to learn is that advanced academic writing is beautiful. The perfect details of the research method, the perfect clarity about quoted words, the power it gives you to develop and communicate important thoughts, even the crisp look of the sentences on the page—it is all beautiful.

Notice: the title is not just "Mary Shelley"; it is an

Otait 1

Ann Otait

Ms. Givvings

English Honors II

18 May 2008

Mary Shelley's Reversal: The Monster Is the Person

Perhaps the greatest surprise to readers who have only seen films of the Frankenstein story is that the book's monster is not the clumsy, staggering oaf of the flickering screen. Instead, the modern Prometheus of Mary Shelley's novel Frankenstein is agile of foot and quick of mind. In fact the humane monster is so intelligent and eager for knowledge that he educates himself in secrecy without his teachers knowing it.

The monster's earliest memories do not indicate unusual intelligence:

> It is with considerable difficulty that I remember the original era of my being; all the events of that period appear confused and indistinct. A strange multiplicity of sensations seized me, and I saw, felt, heard, and smelt, at the same time; and it was, indeed, a long time before I learned to distinguish between the operations of my various senses. (Shelley 106)

Little by little the pitiful monster pulls himself together and begins wandering through the forest, where he learns about the world. One day he discovers a fire left by wandering beggars and learns the joy of being warm. Finding a village, he tries to enter a small hut, but the inhabitants scream, and the villagers chase him away.

In flight he spies a hovel where he takes refuge. Soon he realizes that the hovel is inhabited and that he can secretly occupy an outer storage room, safe from the rain or snow. He begins to secretly observe the family that lives within and discovers that there is an old man, a young girl, and a young man residing there.

This is a split infinitive. The adverb should not split the infinitive to observe.

One day as the monster is peeking through a crack in the wall, the girl takes a musical instrument from a drawer and gives it to the old man. The result is the monster's first musical experience:

> . . . she sat down beside the old man, who, taking up an instrument, began to play, and to produce sounds, sweeter than the voice of the thrush or the nightingale. It was a lovely sight, even to me, poor wretch! who had never beheld aught beautiful before. The silver hair and benevolent countenance of the aged cottager, won my reverence; while the gentle manners of the girl enticed my love. He played a sweet mournful air . . . I felt sensations of a peculiar and overpowering nature; they were a mixture of pain and pleasure, such as I had never experienced, either from hunger or cold, warmth or food; and I withdrew from the window, unable to bear these emotions. (112)

When we quote the previous source again, we only need page number.

This is not the brute monster of popular films; the monster of the book is sweet, and pitiful--perhaps the most human character of the story. Soon the monster begins to care about his new family, even though they are unaware of his presence. He begins doing chores for them, such as gathering firewood.

One day the monster makes one of the great discoveries of his life; he realizes that the sounds made by his friends make words: "By degrees I made a discovery of still greater moment. I found that these people possessed a method of communicating their experience and feelings to one another by articulate sounds" (117). The monster understands that these sounds are things of great importance to the people: "I perceived that the words they spoke sometimes produced pleasure or pain, smiles or sadness, in the minds and countenances of the hearers. This was indeed a godlike science, and I ardently desired to become acquainted with it" (117). For

Otait 3

an entire winter, the peeping monster secretly observes this godlike science, language, learning words such as fire, milk, bread, and wood. He learns father, and sister, and good. He learns dearest. He grows fonder of his surrogate family with each passing day.

Words as such must be underlined.

Eventually the monster observes the young man taking up a book and reading to the old man and the girl. It is a miracle; the reading:

> . . . had puzzled me extremely at first; but, by degrees, I discovered that he uttered many of the same sounds when he read as when he talked. I conjectured, therefore, that he found on the paper signs for speech which he understood, and I ardently longed to comprehend these also. (118)

Notice the good balance between the student's words and the quotations.

Time passes until one day the monster is out collecting food and happens upon a portmanteau containing some books: Milton's Paradise Lost, a volume of Plutarch's Lives, and Goethe's romantic Sorrows of Werter. They are written in the language that the monster has learned and he eagerly returns to his hiding place with his new books: "The possession of these treasures gave me extreme delight; I now continually studied and exercised my mind upon these histories, whilst my friends were employed in their ordinary occupations" (132).

Beginning with a "confused and indistinct" awareness, the pitiful monster of Mary Shelley's imagination explores the world, learns feelings of affection for a human family, becomes enthralled by music, becomes aware of the wonder of language, works to develop a vocabulary, and becomes a self-taught passionate reader. Unlike the stumbling wretch of the motion pictures, the monster of the novel is more human in many ways than the cruel human beings who ostracize him.

Otait 4

Works Cited

Shelley, Mary Wollstonecraft. Frankenstein: Or, the Modern Prometheus. Berkeley, U of California P, 1984.

Gaining Perspective: A Perfect Form

At first it may seem that a three-page academic paper is a huge assignment, that there is an endless amount of writing to be done. Actually, when we type a three-page academic paper in ten-point Courier type font, double-spaced, there is not very much writing required.

Look at the next page. If we take all of the words of our three-page paper on Frankenstein, and shrink them down to a smaller size, we can fit the entire paper on one page. Now we see that the three-page Frankenstein paper only has nine paragraphs, including three long quotations and three short quotations. The paper has about 850 words, about forty sentences.

A three-page paper is little; you will have to make your case quickly.

Therefore, as we work on our papers, we are not in pursuit of big topics. Rather, we are in pursuit of perfect details, so we will select small ideas that can be discussed in a handful of paragraphs and quotes. What we are learning is *correct form* that we can use in any class.

It is not scale that is the problem; it is high quality. We must learn to write in a way that is mistake-free, clear, beautiful, and meaningful. In Chapter 3 let us review some of the rules that make the English in a paper perfect.

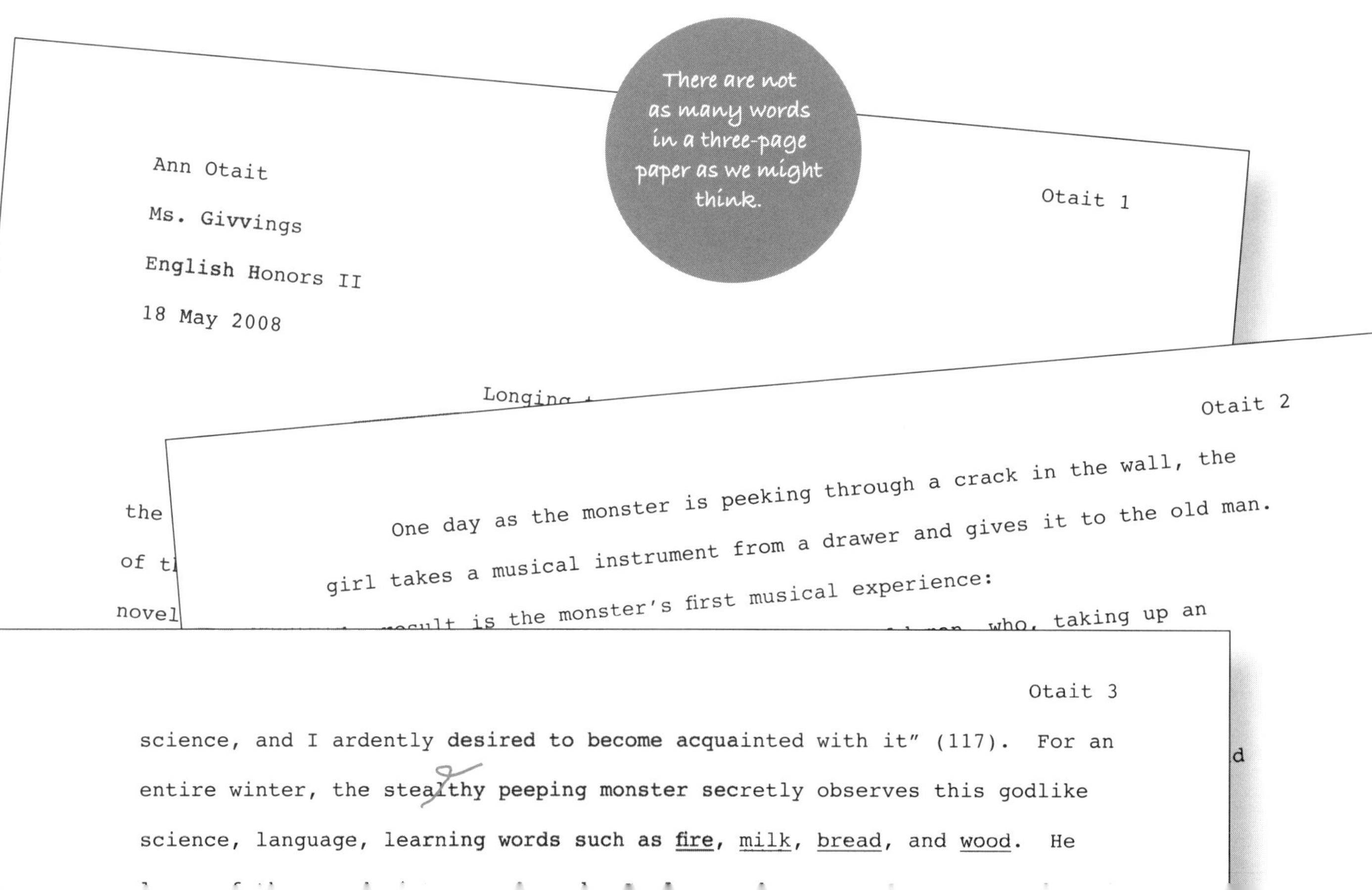

Ann Otait

Ms. Givvings

English Honors II

18 May 2008

Otait 1

Otait 2

One day as the monster is peeking through a crack in the wall, the girl takes a musical instrument from a drawer and gives it to the old man. The result is the monster's first musical experience:

Otait 3

science, and I ardently desired to become acquainted with it" (117). For an entire winter, the stealthy peeping monster secretly observes this godlike science, language, learning words such as fire, milk, bread, and wood. He

This is the entire three-page paper, reduced to five-point type. Our assignments are about quality, not quantity.

Otait 1

Ann Otait

Ms. Givvings

English Honors II

18 May 2008

Mary Shelley's Reversal: The Monster Is the Person

Perhaps the greatest surprise to readers who have only seen films of the Frankenstein story is that the monster is not the clumsy, staggering oaf of the flickering screen. Instead, the modern Prometheus of Mary Shelley's novel Frankenstein is agile of foot and quick of mind. In fact the humane monster is so intelligent and eager for knowledge that he educates himself in secrecy, without his teachers knowing it.

The monster's earliest memories do not reflect unusual intelligence:

> It is with considerable difficulty that I remember the original era of my being; all the events of that period appear confused and indistinct. A strange multiplicity of sensations seized me, and I saw, felt, heard, and smelt, at the same time; and it was, indeed, a long time before I learned to distinguish between the operations of my various senses. (Shelley 106)

Little by little the pitiful monster pulls himself together and begins wandering through the forest, where he learns about the world. One day he discovers a fire left by wandering beggars and learns the joy of being warm. Finding a village, he tries to enter a small hut, but the inhabitants scream, and the villagers chase him away.

In flight he spies a hovel where he takes refuge. Soon, he realizes that the hovel is inhabited, and that he can secretly occupy an outer storage room, safe from the rain or snow. He begins observing the family that lives within, and discovers that there is an old man, a young girl, and a young man residing there.

One day as the monster is peeking through a crack in the wall the girl takes a musical instrument from a drawer and gives it to the old man. The result is the monster's first musical experience:

> . . . she sat down beside the old man, who, taking up an instrument, began to play, and to produce sounds, sweeter than the voice of the thrush or the nightingale. It was a lovely sight, even to me, poor wretch! who had never beheld aught beautiful before. The silver hair and benevolent countenance of the aged cottager, won my reverence; while the gentle manners of the girl enticed my love. He played a sweet mournful air . . . I felt sensations of a peculiar and overpowering nature; they were a mixture of pain and pleasure, such as I had never experienced, either from hunger or cold, warmth or food; and I withdrew from the window, unable to bear these emotions. (112)

This is not the brute monster of popular films; the monster of the book is sweet and pitiful--perhaps the most human character of the story. Soon, the monster begins to care about his new family, even though they are unaware of his presence. He begins doing chores for them, such as gathering firewood.

One day, the monster makes one of the great discoveries of his life; he realizes that the sounds made by his friends make words: "By degrees I made a discovery of still greater moment. I found that these people possessed a method of communicating their experience and feelings to one another by articulate sounds" (117). The monster understands that these sounds are things of great importance to the people: "I perceived that the words they spoke sometimes produced pleasure or pain, smiles or sadness, in the minds and countenances of the hearers. This was indeed a godlike science, and I ardently desired to become acquainted with it" (117). For an entire winter, the peeping monster secretly observes this godlike science, language, learning words such as fire, milk, bread, and wood. He learns father, and sister, and good. He learns dearest. He grows fonder of his surrogate family with each passing day.

Eventually, the monster observes the young man taking up a book and reading to the old man and the girl. It is a miracle:

> This reading had puzzled me extremely at first; but, by degrees, I discovered that he uttered many of the same sounds when he read as when he talked. I conjectured, therefore, that he found on the paper signs for speech which he understood, and I ardently longed to comprehend these also. (118)

Time passes, until one day the monster is out collecting food and happens upon a portmanteau, containing some books: Milton's Paradise Lost, a volume of Plutarch's Lives, and Goethe's romantic Sorrows of Werter. They are written in the language that the monster has learned, and he eagerly returns to his hiding place with his new books: "The possession of these treasures gave me extreme delight; I now continually studied and exercised my mind upon these histories, whilst my friends were employed in their ordinary occupations" (132).

Beginning with a "confused and indistinct" awareness, the pitiful monster of Mary Shelley's imagination explores the world, learns feelings of affection for a human family, becomes enthralled by music, becomes aware of the wonder of language, works to develop a vocabulary, and becomes a self-taught passionate reader. Unlike the plodding monster of the motion pictures, the monster of the novel is more human in many ways than the cruel human beings who reject him.

Works Cited

Shelley, Mary Wollstonecraft. Frankenstein: Or, the Modern Prometheus. Berkeley, U of California P, 1984.

Otait 4

ted

in: Or, the Modern Prometheus.

3. Standard Punctuation, Usage, and Grammar Rules

Punctuation Rules Are Based on Grammar

Every sentence you ever write must be punctuated, and in advanced academic writing there are standard punctuation rules that are enforced, *based on the grammar* of the sentence. If you do not know your basic grammar, you will be unable to punctuate correctly; grammar is required. Rather than put these punctuation and usage rules at the end of the book as a reference section, let us look at them now, before we begin writing. We will put a blue pencil (✎) beside the punctuation rules that are most likely to be important in our papers.

comma: (,)

after introductory participial phrases: `Falling quickly, the chicken clucked.`
after introductory interjections: `Yes, I have no chickens.`
after informal salutations: `Dear Dante, we need more chickens.`
after long introductory prepositional phrases:
`In the chill early wind, the battle chickens attacked.`

✎ **after multiple introductory prepositional phrases:**
`At the beginning of the century, the chickens were in disarray.`

✎ **after introductory dependent clauses (D,I):** `If you go, the chicken goes.`
after the day and year: `January 3, 1987, was a cold day for chickens.`
after the city and state: `Florence, Italy, is the place for chickens.`
around nonessential (nonrestrictive) clauses:
`The chicken, which had a nice smile, turned back.`
around nonessential participial phrases:
`My friend, laughing with delight, produced the pullet.`

✎ **around most appositives:** `Linus Pullet, the Nobel Prize winner, squawked.`
around nouns of direct address: `Yes, Hennypenny, I will.`
around parenthetical expressions: `The chicken will, I hope, squawk.`

✎ **before coordinating conjunctions in I,ccI compound sentences:**
`Dickens wrote novels, and Leghorn wrote poems.`

✎ **between all items in a list:** `The chicken was tall, handsome, and smart`

✎ **between *coordinate* adjectives preceding a noun:** `It's a smart, older chicken.`
between contrasts introduced by *not*: `The chicken is here, not there.`
between name and degree or title: `Marcus Fowlius, Ph.D.`
inside closing quotation marks: `"Shut up," the chicken explained.`

✎ **NOT between *cumulative* adjectives preceding a noun:** `I saw two blue chickens.`
NOT after a short prepositional phrase: `In May the chicken departed.`
NOT between compound subjects/predicates: `Hamlet and Ophelia saw chickens.`
NOT between subject and verb: Wrong: `My good chicken, is here.`

semicolon: (;)

✎ **between independent clauses if no coordinating conjunction: I;I**

`I am a chicken expert; Ben Rogers is a neophyte.`

between items in a list if the items themselves contain commas:

`We ordered bacon; fried, scrambled, and poached eggs; and grits.`

between independent clauses joined by *however*, etc.

`We all wanted to go; however, only the chicken departed.`

colon: (:)

before a list that is not a compound direct object or subject complement:

`There are three kinds: cowards, poltroons, and chickens.`

before a long formal statement: `To hens it may concern:`

✎ **before a long quotation, as in a research paper.**

between hours and minutes in time: `6:15`

between Bible chapter and verse: `Luke 4:16`

after formal salutations: `Dear Mr. Gallinaceous:`

✎ **between titles and subtitles:** Walt Whitman: Poet of America

EVERY sentence must be punctuated, so these standards are crucial.

italics: (no *or no*) (italics and underlining are the same thing)

Use italics when your font is *Times*, and use underline when it is Courier.

Times looks good in italics. Courier looks better underlined.

✎ **title of a book:** *A Tale of Two Chickens*, Chicken Island

✎ **title of a magazine:** *Life* National Geographic

title of a work of art: *Mona Lisa* David

title of a train or airplane: *Spirit of St. Louis* The Hindenberg

✎ **words, letters, and numbers as such:** `the word` blubber, the letter *a*, and the number *5*

foreign language words: *dejà vu*

quotation marks: (" ")

around a direct quotation: `He said, "I am not a chicken."`

commas and periods go inside quotes: `"Too many chickens," he said.`

colons and semicolons go outside quotes: `Foghorn said, "Hi"; I left.`

title of short story, poem, song: `"The Roost Not Taken"`

✎ **title of article, chapter, or part of publication:**

`The fourth chapter of` My False Demise `is entitled "Rumors."`

NOT to indicate cute, trite, or ungrammatical terms:

`Hi, "Buddies," how about a "pep talk!"`

apostrophe: (')

noun made into a possessive: `John's chicken`
missing letter in a contraction: `don't`
missing number in a year contraction: '47
plurals of letters, numbers, signs, and words as such: *a*'s *5*'s

✎ **with an *s* to show possession after a singular noun:** `Charles Chickens's novel`
Note that singular nouns ending in *s* still add '*s*: `Squawkrates's philosophy`
alone to show possession after a plural noun ending in *s*: `dogs'`
for quotations within quotations:
`John said, "Hamlet cried, 'Oops!' when he fell."`

✎ **in the contraction of *it* and *is*:** `It's a very fine chicken.`
NOT in the possessive pronoun *its*.

✎ **NOT in plural centuries or decades:** `1900s  the 50s`

hyphen: (-)

word divided at end of line
compound written numbers from twenty-one to ninety-nine
fractions used as adjectives: `a three-fourths majority`
prefixes before proper noun or proper adjective: `Pre-Raphaelite`
compound nouns that include prepositional phrases: `father-in-law`
compound adjective when it precedes its noun: `a well-meant lie`
NOT in compound adjectives after nouns: `It was well meant.`
do NOT use a hyphen (-) **when you intend a dash** (-- or —)

dash: (-- or —)

A dash is twice as long as a hyphen. Hyphen: - Dash: —

✎ **abrupt break in thought:** `So I--wait a minute!--ate the fish.`

✎ **Make a dash in Courier or on a typewriter with** `two hyphens, NO spaces--thus.`
NOT to replace proper punctuation.

ellipsis: (. . .)

✎ **to indicate words omitted from quotations**
In Courier the ellipsis is made of five spaces and three periods:
`There are blank spaces between the periods . . . see?`
Use three periods if the omission is within a sentence.
Use four periods if the omission includes sentence ending.

parenthesis: (( ))

around parenthetical remarks added to a sentence:
`He said I would be (I wish!) six feet tall.`

brackets: ([ ])

around words inserted into quoted material:

Johnson notes, "At this time [Dickens] began to weaken."

When you insert words into quotations—usually for the purpose of clarifying references or enhancing the flow of the sentences—you must enclose your inserted words in brackets like [this] to show that these words were not part of the original quote. Be sure to use true [brackets] rather than (parentheses) or <mathematical symbols>.

question mark: (?)

at the end of an interrogative sentence: Do you have chickens?
inside closing quotes if part of quote: Tybalt asked, "Are there chickens?"
outside quotes if not part of quote: Did the ghost say, "Remember my chicken"?

period: (.)

at the end of a declarative sentence: I have three chickens.
at the end of a mild imperative sentence: Please pursue the chicken.
after most abbreviations: Dr. Trelawney saw the chicken.
inside closing quotation marks: He said, "Stop that chicken."

exclamation point: (!)

after an exclamatory sentence: The sky is falling!
after a strong imperative sentence: All chickens leave the room!
NOT to be cute: Hi! Guess what!!

Study the rules; do what you must to learn the real rules of punctuation.

Otait 1

Ann Otait

Ms. Givvings

English Honors II

18 May 2008

Longing to Comprehend:

The Frankenstein Monster's Self-education

Perhaps the greatest surprise to readers who have only seen films of the Frankenstein story is that the monster is not the clumsy, staggering oaf of the flickering screen. Instead, the modern Prometheus of Mary Shelleys' novel Frankenstein is agile of foot and quick of mind. In fact the humane monster is so intelligent and eager for knowledge that he educates himself without his teachers knowing it.

...ual intelligence:

A Punctuation Challenge

In advanced academic writing, punctuation rules are serious. We might ignore punctuation in our private diary, but in a paper that we submit for a grade in an academic class, we follow the real rules. For the most part, these rules are not flexible; they are not subject to personal preference or feeling. We might punctuate a novel or a poem with some degree of flexibility, but advanced academic writing—formal writing—permits little personal flexibility in punctuation.

Consider this: *every* sentence you write must be punctuated. You will never write a sentence that does not use one or more of the rules on the previous four pages. This means that in academic writing, the punctuation of every sentence is either correct or incorrect. If you do not know how to punctuate your grammar, your mistakes will add up, fast. This in turn means that you must devote yourself to learning the details of standard punctuation, and you must work on it until you have it absolutely mastered.

The Works Cited page below has five punctuation errors. Can you find them? The example on the following page shows the disaster that can happen when someone does not know how to punctuate. For all of its accomplishments, the one page contains twenty punctuation errors, so it must receive a failing grade. Can you find the twenty errors?

Why does advanced academic writing demand perfection in elementary grammar, punctuation, and mechanics? Little details are big deals because when little details are perfect, then all of the attention can shift to the important ideas, and our minds are free to think about truth.

For three quizzes that will help teach punctuation, see the teacher section at the end of the book.

Find Five Errors

Otait 4

Works Cited

Cartledge, Paul. Alexander the Great. New York: Overlook, 2004.

Cummings, Lewis V. Alexander the Great. New York, Grove, 1968.

Fox, Robin Lane Alexander the Great. New York: Penguin, 2004.

Green, Peter. Alexander of Macedon, 356-323 B.C.: A Historical Biography. Berkeley: U. of California P, 1991.

Rogers, Guy MacLean. Alexander: The Ambiguity of Greatness. New York: Random, 2004

Find Twenty Errors

Suggestion: let students work in small groups, open-book, to find the errors.

Otait, 1

Ann Otait

Ms. Givvings

English Honors

18 May 2008

Longing to Comprehend:

The Frankenstein Monsters Self-education

Perhaps the greatest surprise to readers who have only seen films of the Frankenstein story is that the monster is not the clumsy, staggering oaf of the flickering screen. Instead, the modern Prometheus of Mary Shelley's novel Frankenstein is agile of foot, and quick of mind. In fact, the humane monster is so intelligent, optimistic and eager for knowledge that he educates himself in secrecy, without his teachers knowing it.

The monsters' earliest memories do not reflect unusual intelligence:

> Its with considerable difficulty that I remember the original era of my being; all the events of that period appear confused and indistinct. A strange multiplicity...seized me, and I saw, felt, heard, and smelt, at the same time; it was, indeed, a long time before I learned to distinguish between the operations of my various senses (Shelley, 106).

This period should be after senses, followed by two blank spaces.

Little by little the pitiful monster, pulls himself together, and begins wandering through the forest, where he learns about the world. One day he discovers a fire left by wandering beggars, and learns the joy of being warm. Finding a village, he tries to enter a small hut but the inhabitants scream, and the villagers, chase him away.

In flight he spies a hovel and he takes refuge. When he realizes that the hovel is inhabited he secretly occupies it's outer storage room, safe from the rain and snow. He begins observing the family that lives within, and discovers that there is an old man, a young girl and a young man who

Common English Usage Problems.

Here is a list of common problems in English grammar and usage. Read this list carefully and then refer back to it when you are writing. Give special notice to items marked with pencils.

To **accept** is to take: I can accept no money for this chicken.
To **except** is to omit: I can except no one from the rule except you or that chicken.

✎ The verb **affect** means to influence: Your chicken will affect many people.
The verb **effect** means cause: Your chicken will effect a new procedure.
The noun **effect** means result: Your chicken will produce a good effect.

✎ It is best to use the word **impact** only as a noun, and not as a verb, in discussing the effect of individuals on history. When we say that x "impacted" y, this usage has an unfortunate, unpleasant medical connotation that is undesirable. The preferable word is **affected**. We affect others, rather than impact them, and when we affect them, this has an impact.

Use **afraid of** and **frightened by**, rather than **frightened of**: He was frightened by a chicken, and was afraid of them ever since.

To **aggravate** is to make worse, not to irritate: It irritated her that she aggravated her cold. In other words we should not say, "That insult aggravated me."

✎ Use **all right**, **not alright**: We will be all right if the chickens arrive.

Use **a lot**, not **alot**. That is a lot of chickens.

An **allusion** is a reference: His comment was an allusion to the chicken in the *Iliad*.
An **illusion** is a deception: The bas relief of the chicken gave the illusion of depth.

Use **and**, not **&.** In ordinary sentences, do not substitute the ampersand (**&**) or the mathematical plus symbol (**+**) for the coordinating conjunction *and*.

Bad is an adjective: The bad decision ruined the chicken.
Badly is an adverb: The bad chicken did not swim badly.

✎ The reason is not **because**; the reason is **that**: The reason we hesitate is that we remember.

Something is **between** two: This secret is between you and the chicken.
Something is **among** three or more: Divide the fish among the five chickens.

We **bring** toward, but we **take** away: If you take someone's chicken by mistake, you must bring it back to him or her.

Can means able to: You can repair a chicken if you know how.
May means are permitted to: Yes, you may leave the chicken.

✎ Not **could of** or **should of**, but **could have** or **should have**: I could have chased chickens, and I should have chased chickens.

Disinterested means without prejudice because of having no personal interest in something: We need a disinterested judge to try this case fairly. **Uninterested** means without interest in the sense of being bored: The chicken was uninterested in the disinterested judge.

Use **done** only with a helping verb: I **have done** nothing to the chicken.

Don't is the contraction of "do not": We don't like chickens.
Doesn't is the contraction of "does not": He doesn't like chickens.
Don't use **don't** for singular subjects: Wrong: He don't like chickens.

To **emigrate** is to migrate out: The chicken emigrated from Russia.
To **immigrate** is to migrate in: The chicken immigrated to Puerto Rico.

Use **farther** for distance: Her chicken went farther than his did.
Use **further** for time: We will consider this chicken further.

One page at a time, ask students which error is most surprising to them.

Use **feel bad** rather than **feel badly**: The chicken felt bad.

Use **fewer** for countable things: There are fewer chickens.
Use **less** for uncountable amount: There is less sugar for the chickens.

✎ If you are enumerating elements in your essay, use **first** and **second**, rather than *firstly* and *secondly*. The latter terms with their *-ly* suffix have a supercilious, pedantic ring to them that is undesirable.

Fortuitous means by chance: A fortuitous circumstance occurred with the chicken.
Fortunate means lucky: A fortunate condition resulted for the chickens.

Good is an adjective: The good chicken swam her fastest time.
Well is usually an adverb: The good chicken swam well.
Well can sometimes be an adjective: He is not a well chicken.

Clothes, when put out to dry, are **hung**. People, when strung up to die, are **hanged**.

✎ **Hopefully** is an adverb meaning "full of hope"; it should not be used as a substitute for I hope. To say "Hopefully, I can go," is an error.

Ideas are concepts, thoughts, and so forth. We could discuss the philosophical ideas of Friedrich Nietzsche. **Ideals** are standards, goals to be attained, ideas of perfection.

To **imply** is to suggest: He implied that chickens were to blame.
To **infer** is to deduce: We inferred that chickens were being blamed.

✎ **It's** is the contraction of **it is**: It's fun to understand chickens.
Its is a possessive pronoun: The chicken chomped its beak.

Use **kind of** rather than **kind of a**: It seemed to be some kind of nose.

Use **lend** as a verb: Lend me money for a chicken.
Use **loan** as a noun: Give me a loan for a chicken.

Ask students which error on each page is the most common.

To **lie** (v.i.) is to rest: I will lie here in the shade near the chickens.
To **lay** (v.t.) is to put: I will lay the hammer here near the chicken.

Use **like** as a preposition: We have good chickens like these.
Use **as** as a conjunction: We have good chickens, as you have.

✎ **Literally** means actually, not figuratively. You could say, "We literally left within two minutes," but not, "We literally vanished." If you did not really physically vanish, you did not literally vanish. Literally means really.

In the past we used the terms **man** and **mankind**, and even the possessive pronoun **his**, to refer to all human beings, both male and female. Today, our sensitivities have improved, and we try to avoid defaulting to the masculine gender when we intend to express something which also includes women. Other terms, such as **human beings**, **humanity**, **persons**, and even the compound pronouns such as **his or her** sound more accurate and more fair.

Myself and **yourself** should be used as reflexive or intensive pronouns rather than as direct objects. "I, myself, believed the chicken" is correct usage, but "She asked John and myself if we had the chicken" is not. It would be correct to say, "She asked John and me if we had the chicken."

Nauseous means sickening: The chicken was nauseous to us.
Nauseated means sick at the stomach: The seasick chicken was nauseated.
In other words, if I say "I am nauseous," it means I make *you* sick. When my stomach is upset, I am nauseated, not nauseous.

Number is for countables: There were a number of chickens there.
Amount is for uncountables: There was an enormous amount of tension among the flock of white chickens.

Use **off** rather than **off of**: The ball bounced off the backboard near the chicken.

Use **more than**, not **over; over** means above or on top of; it does not mean *more than*.

✎ **Phenomenon** is singular and **phenomena** is plural: The weirdest phenomenon was the tornado.

✎ Save **plus** for mathematics and use **in addition to** or **also** in most other situations.

Precipitate means hasty, and **precipitous** means steep.

✎ The phrase **relate to** is a vague colloquialism. Instead of saying that many people relate to J.D. Salinger's character Holden Caulfield, say that many people understand Holden, or that they find that Holden's struggles remind them of their own struggles.

Use **raise** transitively: The chickens will attempt to raise the Titanic.
Use **rise** intransitively: The chicken began to rise slowly through the air.

Use **regardless** rather than **irregardless**.

Respectfully is with respect: He spoke respectfully of his chicken.
Respectively is in sequence: He spoke of his father, his brother, and his chicken, respectively.

Use **since** rather than **seeing as how**: Since you feel that way, I will find the chicken myself.

You **sit** (v.i.) down in a chair: She was sitting there near the chicken.
You **set** (v.t.) down a book: She was setting the chicken on the step.

Someone is not they. Rather than saying, "Someone dropped *their* headphones," say, "Someone dropped a pair of headphones." Use **they** or **their** only if you mean a group of people.

You **teach** people things, and you **learn** subjects: you do NOT learn people things.

✎ **Than** is a conjunction: We have more chickens than you have.
Then is an adverb: We will go now; you go then.

Them should be used as an object pronoun, not as an adjective: And so, my friends, ask not when you can have them chickens, ask when you can have those chickens.

They're is the contraction of "they are": They're feeding chickens now.
Their is a possessive pronoun: They're feeding their chickens.
There is a place: They're feeding their chickens there.

To is a preposition or an infinitive: She went to Boston to think about chickens.
Too is an adverb meaning "also" or "too much": I sleep too much, too.
Two is a number: Two chickens twisted twine in the twilight.

Use **try to** rather than **try and**: Please try to help the chickens.

Something is either **unique**, one of a kind, or it is not. There are no degrees of uniqueness, and so nothing can be *very* unique. The plastic chicken is unique.

Use **use**, not **utilize**. He used a plastic owl to frighten the chickens.

Use **way off** rather than **ways off**: He was a long way off from the chickens.

Who is a subject pronoun: Who is with the chickens?
Whom is an object pronoun: To whom do you wish give the chickens?

Who refers to people: It was they who followed the chicken.
That and **which** refer to objects: Which chicken is that?

Who's is the contraction of *who* and *is*. Who's going to think about the chickens?
Whose is a pronoun or adjective: Whose chickens these are, I think I know.

The sample on the next page has ten serious grammar or usage errors. Can you find all ten?

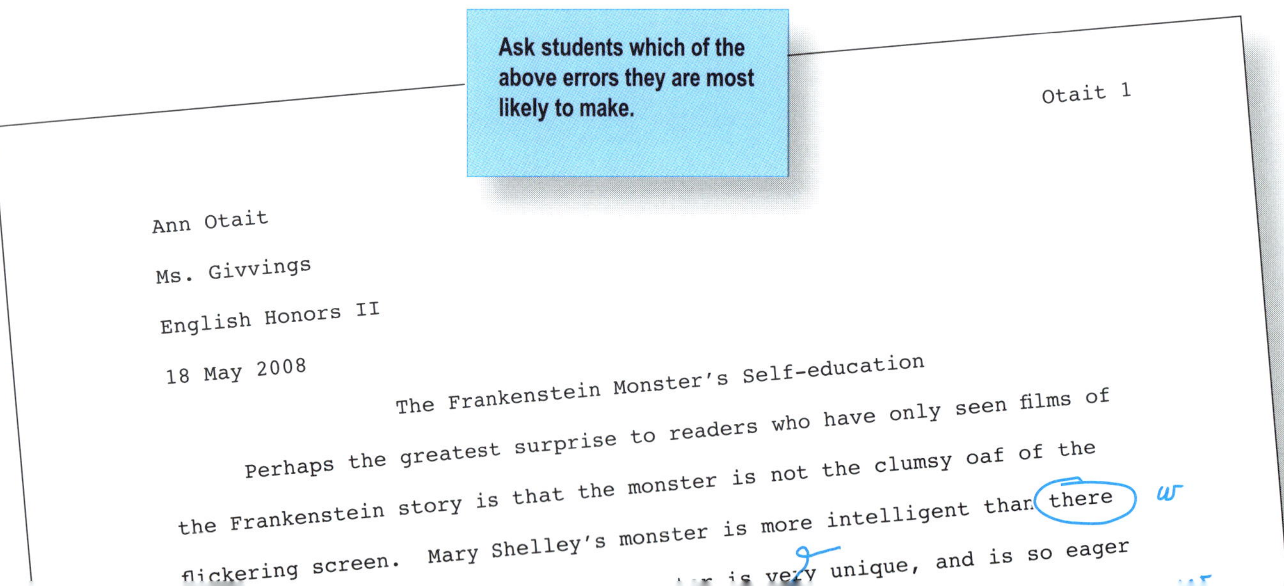

Otait 1

Ann Otait

Ms. Givvings

English Honors II

18 May 2008

The Frankenstein Monster's Self-education

Perhaps the greatest surprise to readers who have only seen films of the Frankenstein story is that the monster is not the clumsy oaf of the flickering screen. Mary Shelley's monster is more intelligent than there ... is very unique, and is so eager

Find Ten Usage Errors

In formal, standard English, we avoid usage errors.

Otait 1

Ann Otait

Ms. Givvings

English Honors II

18 May 2008

Longing to Comprehend:

The Frankenstein Monster's Self-education

Perhaps what most impacts readers who have only seen films of the Frankenstein story is that the monster is not the clumsy, staggering phenomena of the flickering screen. Instead, the modern Prometheus of Mary Shelley's novel Frankenstein is agile of foot and quick of mind. In fact the humane monster is to intelligent and eager for knowledge; he educates himself in secrecy and is more intelligent then the human beings.

The monster's earliest memories do not reflect unusual intelligence:

> It is with considerable difficulty that I remember the original era of my being; all the events of that period appear confused and indistinct. A strange multiplicity of sensations seized me, and I saw, felt, heard, and smelt, at the same time; and it was, indeed, a long time before I learned to distinguish between the operations of my various senses. (Shelley 106)

Little by little the pitiful monster pulls himself together and begins wandering through the forest, where he wants to try and learn about the world. One day he discovers a fire left by wandering beggars and decides to learn there customs. Finding a village, he tries to enter a small hut, but the inhabitants scream, and over fifty villagers are frightened of him and chase him away. He wishes he could of made friends with them.

In flight he spies a hovel where he takes refuge. Soon he realizes that the hovel is inhabited, and he begins observing it's inhabitants. He discovers that there is an old man, a young girl, and a young man who

Ten Common English Grammar Problems

This is not a grammar textbook, but correct grammar is a vital element of advanced academic writing. For a full-fledged grammar program, see *The Magic Lens, Volume One*, but because grammar is so integral to good writing, let us at least review ten of the most troublesome grammar errors. We will make thumbnail comments here, including proofreader's marks in blue, and expand the ideas later when we come to the writing assignments.

Subject / Verb Disagreement s/v

The subject/verb disagreement is the worst error in grammar. The subject of each sentence with be either singular or plural, and the verb must agree with it in number. If the subject is singular, the verb must be singular.

Wrong: The reason for the numerous objections are obvious.

Right: The reason for the numerous objections is obvious.

Sentence Fragment frag

Advanced academic writing is made of complete sentences. Groups of words that do not make complete thoughts are errors.

Wrong: When scientists first photographed the squid. They were amazed.

Right: When scientists first photographed the squid, they were amazed.

Run-On Sentence R-S

A compound sentence joined by a coordinating conjunction must have a comma before the conjunction, or else it is a run-on sentence.

Wrong: The sun began to rise slowly and they saw the extent of the damage.

Right: The sun began to rise slowly, and they saw the extent of the damage.

Pronoun Case pron

Subjects and subject complements must use subject pronouns. Direct objects, indirect objects, objects of prepositions, and objects of verbals must use object pronouns.

Wrong: It will be important to you and I.

Right: It will be important to you and me.

To write academic papers, you MUST know your grammar. Do you need to review?

Pronoun Reference ref

When multiple nouns precede a pronoun, the antecedent of the pronoun can become unclear.

Wrong: James suddenly encountered John, and he looked startled.

Right: James suddenly encountered John, and John looked startled.

A *They/Their* Error ref

The pronouns *they* and *their* are plural, not singular. When something is *theirs*, then it belongs to a group. Something belonging to an individual is *his* or *hers*.

Wrong: One of the poets dropped their book.

Right: One of the poets dropped a book.

Misplaced Modifier mm

An introductory participial phrase must be set off by a comma and must modify the grammatical subject of the sentence.

Wrong: Barking furiously at the mailman, Susan shushed Fido.

Right: Barking furiously at the mailman, Fido angered Susan.

Split Infinitive We would use the delete mark to remove the inserted word.

We regard an infinitive as a single word. In advanced academic writing we do not split the infinitive with an adverb.

Wrong: Roosevelt began to slowly develop economic programs.

Right: Slowly, Roosevelt began to develop economic programs.

Parallel lists and compounds //

Lists and compounds need to be constructed with parallel grammar. A list should consist of all adjectives or all nouns, but not a mixture.

Wrong: Dickens was a novelist, a poet, and spoke often.

Right: Dickens was a novelist, a poet, and a frequent public speaker.

Parallel Tense t

Tenses should not wander; they should be logical. If you are describing the past, stay in past tense.

Wrong: Jefferson went home. Soon he is building again.

Right: Jefferson went home. Soon he was building again.

4. Core-Element Grading

Grading that is not a distraction.

Writing should be a creative joy, and yet we all remember times when we were trying to learn important knowledge, but we also wanted to get a good grade, and the complicated grading system distracted us, making it hard to focus on the knowledge. The knowledge was one thing, and the grading was something else, and it distracted our thought.

This can be true with writing. To write well, we need a laser-focus on the few core elements of writing, and yet to get good grades we sometimes have to navigate the hubbub of an elaborate point system where this error is one point, that error is two points, this category is worth twenty-five points . . . it all begins to seem like a mathematical accounting process instead of a human writing experience. In order to get a good grade in a system like that, we may not be able to think like real writers at all. Good writing requires a clear, writer's mind.

Perhaps in a perfect world grading would be unnecessary, and we could teach and learn without the separate pressure of evaluation. In the real world, alas, schools have to demonstrate in quantifiable ways that students are learning, and sometimes students use the pressure of the grade to motivate them. In most (though not all) school settings, papers are graded.

So if we have to have a grading system for advanced academic writing, how can we set it up so that there is no difference between writer-mind and good-grades-mind? How can we design the grading process so that it does not give us something *else* to think about, that a professional writer would never have to think about? How can we design the grading so that to get a high grade, you have to think like a writer? Here is how: we take the elements that writers have to think about, and build the grade on those elements alone, without introducing any additional, artificial grading system business.

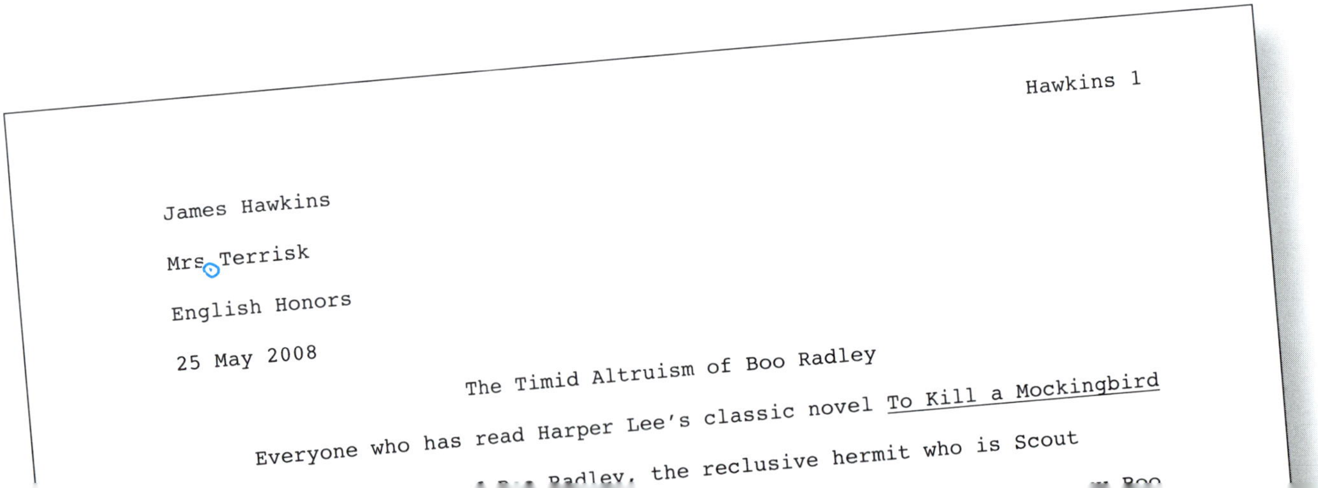

Hawkins 1

James Hawkins

Mrs Terrisk

English Honors

25 May 2008

The Timid Altruism of Boo Radley

Everyone who has read Harper Lee's classic novel To Kill a Mockingbird

Radley, the reclusive hermit who is Scout

How, then, do writers think? First, even though good writers know hundreds of details and rules about punctuation, usage, grammar, style, and form, they do not write with these hundreds of things in their minds at once. The knowledge-cloud of rules stays in the background, visited with quick mental checks by the writer as questions arise. The writer knows those details, but they are so well known that they can wait in the background.

One of the reasons writing can be a joy is that the real writer's mind is not filled with grading grids, extravagant rubrics, point games, or checklists. In a writer's mind there are a few core writing truths, and each is important. These, then, are the concepts upon which we will base our grading. They are what a writer would think about, whether or not the paper was graded. What are these core writing elements? For the advanced academic writing that we will learn, the core elements are few, simple, and obvious:

1. Correct English.
2. Correct MLA format.
3. Correct essay structure.
4. A meaningful idea. This element is the purpose of the first three.

There is nothing artificial or arbitrary about these four elements. They are real; if the writing you submit to your future teachers and professors does not have these qualities, you are in trouble. Yes, each of the four elements can be subdivided into dozens or even hundreds of concrete details, but these are the main concepts that organize all of those details into real writing knowledge.

Once again, your teacher must decide how he or she will grade your papers, but let us imagine our imaginary class, in which I will grade your papers in the strict way that they are often graded in actual high school and college work. In our imaginary class, Here is how I will grade:

If you want a *D* or higher, get your English right.

Either we are serious about advanced academic writing, or we are not. If you want a *D* or a passing grade, then the paper must—at the very least—be at grade-level English. It must be free or almost free of elementary errors of spelling, grammar, punctuation, word usage, and formal style. These papers are not in-class assignments scribbled in an hour; you have time to proofread them, double-checking every detail. A paper filled with bad elementary English should and will receive an *F*, regardless of its other merits. You are responsible for correct elementary English, and this is non-negotiable.

If you want a *C* or higher, also get your MLA format right.

In order to receive a *C*, the paper must not only be in good English, it must also be in correct MLA format. It must have a one-inch, ragged-right margin, be in double-spaced Courier type font, have a mix of long and short quotations done in MLA style, and have a correct Works Cited page. Papers that are not in MLA format are not acceptable and will be returned to be redone. Part of advanced academic writing is following the assigned format.

If you want a *B* or higher, also get your essay structure right.

If your paper is written in good English and is in correct MLA format, then we can look at the third element, the essay structure. In the advanced academic writing of our assignments, you must write a true essay with an introduction, body, and conclusion built around a thesis that connects the paper together. Furthermore, the paragraphs must be unified with language that connects each paragraph to the next or previous paragraph.

If you want an *A*, also have a good thesis.

If you want an *A*, your paper must have four elements: good English, correct MLA format, clear essay form, and finally a worthwhile idea. It must have an interesting, meaningful thesis that is original and insightful and that makes the paper worth reading. This does not mean that the thesis must be a major concept or grand theory—our little three-page papers are too short for that sort of masterpiece—but it means that you must find an interesting and worthwhile insight to talk about in the little space of three pages. You may have to do a considerable amount of reading and thinking before you begin to write.

Let us look at samples of what these different grades might actually look like. We cannot demonstrate every possible variation, but it is worth some time to train our eyes and to begin to detect the elements of advanced writing. For these sample papers, we will not use real books, real authors, or even real publishers. Our imaginary publishing firms will be:

Absalom University Press
Branes and Marble Ltd.
Cheetah Book Publishing Company
Halfcourt Smith and Burns
Randle House, Inc.
University of Epsilon Press

Before you turn the page: how many serious errors can you find in this paper?

Rochipp 1

Mike Rochipp

Ms. Teemornin

English Honors

5 May 2008

Charles Dicken's Life

Charles Dickens was born on Febuary 7, 1812 and he was a awsome writer who we should all admire. Each of his great works have they're own good qualities. As a boy young he always liked to read to and he reads alot of books including The Illiad by Homer a Greek writer When he was young. He was born in Hampshire Englend. His father was locked up in the slammer it was called Marshalsea Debtors Prison. Being a prisoner, Dickens is ashamed because everyone knew about there poverty he has to suddenly work 10 hours every day at a boot blacking factory. And his mother left him their to long which Dickens didn't like. In his interesting book The Little Dickens an author named Jason Flem says these words to explain to you how the prison put it's mark mark on him:

> Charles Dickens early life went from bad to when his father was imprisioned for failure to pay his debts. After several months his fathr was able to leave the prison, but the familys financial status remained bad for some time afterwards until his father inherited money. (Flem 273)

Life slowly past but in 1827 only 3 years later Dickens went to work at a law office called Ellis and Blackmore and he is a junior law clerk where these things that he saw and witnessed in the law firm made him hate the legal profession and he wrote about many bad character's in his novels who were lawyers they didn't care about anybody but themselves. Robert Mandarin said that "Charles Dickens hated lawyers" (Mandarin 78).

When Dickens wrote his novels he showed how people have there dignity,

Rochipp 4

Works Cited

Adams, Jane. The Social and Egalitarian Themes of Charles Dickens's Novels. New York: Halfcourt, 2004.

Drummin, Lazlo V. A Man Who Is Pure at Heart. New York, Absalom UP, 1973

Flem, Jason The Little Dickens. New York: Randel, 2004.

Mandarin, Robert. The Imaginary Concsience of Charles Dickens. Chicago: U of Epsilon P, 2001.

Mike's Paper: the Assessment

On the opposite page is Mike's paper again, this time with errors circled. To his credit Mike tried to get the MLA format right, but his Works Cited page has too many mistakes. The long quote is indented eleven spaces. The topic of the paper, Charles Dickens's life, is too big for a little three-page paper. Worse, the paper is not an essay; Dickens's life is not a thesis, and the first paragraph is not an introduction but a muddle of boring encyclopedia facts.

When we look at Mike's English, we see that the paper cannot get a passing grade, no matter how good the other elements are. The paper is riddled with errors of grammar, spelling, usage, and punctuation, so will be a low *F* or a high *F*, depending upon his MLA format, essay structure, and thesis quality. Look *closely* at these details:

We see serious punctuation errors, such as in the title, where the possessive is *Dicken's* instead of *Dickens's*. By putting the apostrophe in the middle of Dickens's name, Mike has changed the name from *Dickens* to *Dicken*! Mike also puts an apostrophe in the possessive *its* in line eleven. In line twenty-three he forgets to put a comma after an introductory dependent clause.

We see spelling errors (*awsome*,*fathr*), even including the horrific misspelling of one of the great literary masterpieces of the world: Homer's *Iliad*. Mike spells it *Illiad* and forgets to underline the book title. (He also fails to underline the book *The Little Dickens* in line nine and again on the Works Cited page. Remember that in *Times we use italics*, in `Courier underline`.)

Mike uses the numerals *3* and *10* instead of the words *three* and *ten*, which are expected in a formal paper, and he uses sloppy contractions such as *didn't* instead of complete words.

There are fatal grammar errors. Mike makes a subject/verb disagreement error in line two; it should be *each has*, not *each have*. He makes a disastrous misplaced modifier error in line six, with the resultant meaning that Dickens himself was a prisoner! His verb tenses wander illogically from past to present. He uses the adjective *past* instead of the verb *passed* in line seventeen. Mike makes usage mistakes with *there*, *their*, and *they're*, and in line three he uses *to* when he means *too*. He uses *alot* instead of *a lot*. The trendy adjective *awesome* is not appropriate in a formal academic paper.

Rochipp 1

Mike Rochipp

Ms. Teemornin

English Honors

5 May 2008

Charles Dicken's Life

Charles Dickens was born on Febuary 7, 1812 and he was a awsome writer who we should all admire. Each of his great works have they're own good qualities. As a boy young he always liked to read to and he reads alot of books including The Illiad by Homer a Greek writer When he was young. He was born in Hampshire Englend. His father was locked up in the slammer it was called Marshalsea Debtors Prison. Being a prisoner, Dickens is ashamed because everyone knew about there poverty he has to suddenly work 10 hours every day at a boot blacking factory. And his mother left him their to long which Dickens didn't like. In his interesting book The Little Dickens an author named Jason Flem says these words to explain to you how the prison put it's mark mark on him:

> Charles Dickens early life went from bad to when his father was imprisioned for failure to pay his debts. After several months his fathr was able to leave the prison, but the familys financial status remained bad for some time afterwards until his father inherited money. (Flem 273)

Life slowly past but in 1827 only 3 years later Dickens went to work at a law office called Ellis and Blackmore and he is a junior law clerk where these things that he saw and witnessed in the law firm made him hate the legal profession and he wrote about many bad character's in his novels who were lawyers they didn't care about anybody but themselves. Robert Mandarin said that "Charles Dickens hated lawyers" (Mandarin 78).

When Dickens wrote his novels he showed how people have there dignity,

Rochipp 4

Works Cited

Adams, Jane. The Social and Egalitarian Themes of Charles Dickens's Novels. New York: Halfcourt, 2004.

Drummin, Lazlo V. A Man Who Is Pure at Heart. New York, Absalom UP, 1973

Flem, Jason The Little Dickens. New York: Randel, 2004.

Mandarin, Robert. The Imaginary Concsience of Charles Dickens. Chicago: U of Epsilon P, 2001.

Your grade is your doing.

So Mike receives an *F*. Because the concept of an *F* seems so traumatic both to students and to teachers, we should pause to reflect on his grade further. In the first place, there is no reason for any student in a strong English program to receive such a grade, ever. You do not have to receive a failing grade because the English is under your control. When you turn in an unacceptable paper, it is not that the *teacher gives you* that grade; you wrote those mistakes. The teacher is only reporting what you did. No one forced you not to proofread. No one stopped you from looking things up. Advanced academic writing means being academically mature and accepting full personal responsibility for your own English. If you do not accept spelling, punctuation, or grammar errors in your sentences, then they will not be there. The best students have academic pride and academic attitude; they check, and recheck, and recheck their work in major papers because they know that those low-level mistakes are not tolerated. Advanced writing only begins after that level is left behind.

Once we leave elementary English mistakes behind...

Once we leave elementary English mistakes behind, we can concentrate on the real elements of advanced academic writing. As we briefly mentioned before, we immediately confront a stark reality: advanced academic papers are typed. They are not submitted in handwriting.

Sometimes students who are new to this process get someone else (such as a parent, sometimes even a parent's secretary) to type their paper. Almost always, that is a disaster, both short-term and long-term. Why? Short-term, whoever does your work was not in class and did not hear the instructions, so when the paper does not follow the MLA rules and other extra instructions given in the classroom, it has to be returned to the student and redone before it can be graded. "But my parent typed it" is no excuse. Typically there is a letter-grade-per-day penalty assessed. Long-term, having someone else type your papers prevents you from learning to do it; it leaves you dependent, searching for other people to do your work. Especially now that computers are ubiquitous (everywhere), you can and should type your own papers.

So, yes, you will type your own paper; the question is, "How?" That is where the MLA method comes in. As we have seen, the MLA provides the simplest guidelines ever devised for this process. Let us look at another paper, this one submitted by Sarah Connor.

Sarah Connor

English Honors
Mrs. Saranson
May 5, 2008

Emily Dickinson

Born on December 10, 1830, in Amherst, Massachussets, Emily Dickinson would become one of the greatest American poets, even though she was almost completely unknown during her life. Reclusive and taciturn, Dickinson rarely left Amherst, and visited the rest of the world through her imagination:

> Dickinson decked herself in white clothing and rarely left the house. She lived quietly, read Robert Browning's poetry, and took her dog for walks. Any romantic feelings she ever had for anyone came to nothing, and she died unknown and in some ways isolated (Laura Roberson, p. 273).

As a child Dickinson became depressed after a cousin died of typhus. Her emotional condition because serious enough that her parents sent her to Boston to get her out of her environment.

She went to school at Amherst Academy, where she spent seven years studying literature, science, history, mathematics, and Latin. She was ill in 1845 and only attended school for eleven weeks. Her biographer, Ronald Barnes, concluded that Dickinson "attained some of the fundamentals of a true education at Amherst, but not much more than that" (Ronald Barnes, p. 387).

In 1847 Dickinson went to Mount Holyoke Female Seminary, but she only spent ten months there before her brother took her home, and the institution "does not appear to have made a lasting effect on her mind" (Saladin, p. 72). The following year Dickinson busied herself with family and local community life.

Bibliography

Robertson, Laura. (1990) *Emily Dickinson and the Epic Voyage of a Solitary Heart*. New York City: Halfcourt and Bruce Publishing Company.

Barnes, Ronald (2001) *The Evolution of a Major Poet*. Boston: Randel House Inc.

Saladin, Malamud. (1998) *The Genesis Effect: Common Elements in the Lives of Great Creative Minds*. New York: Absalom University Press.

Thomas, Robert. (2007) *The Imaginary Concsience of Charles Dickens*.

Sarah's Paper: the Assessment

Here is Sarah's paper again, but this time mistakes are marked. The elementary English is excellent; her paper contains no spelling, punctuation, usage, or grammar errors. If it is in good MLA form, it can receive a *C* or higher. If it is not an MLA paper, it will be returned to be redone. Is that too extreme?

No. When it comes to a formal standard such as MLA, the details of the format *must be obeyed exactly*. There is no tolerance of deviation, not even in a small detail. This is true not just in the school classroom or in universities but also in publication. If you want to have an article published in a journal, the editors will expect you to submit a correctly formatted article, with every word, letter, space, margin, indentation, and period exactly as the standard states.

What is wrong with Sarah's MLA format? Everything:

It does not have one-inch margins. (Close does not count.)
The right margin is justified instead of ragged-right.
The name and page number header is missing.
The title is not centered, and should not be in bold face.
The title page information is not in the correct place.
The type font is Times Roman instead of Courier. (The teacher required this.)
Paragraphs are not indented exactly five spaces.
The long quotation is not double-spaced, and it is not indented exactly ten spaces.
The period after the long quotation is in the wrong place.
There are blank lines around the long quotation.
The parentheticals are wrong; they have first names, commas, and *p* for page number.
The Works Cited page says *Bibliography* instead of *Works Cited*.
The Works Cited listings are not alphabetized by author's last name.
The Works Cited listings' first lines are indented.
The sequence of the works cited contents is wrong; the date should be last.
The publishers are not abbreviated.

If this paper had been in perfect MLA form, might it have received a *B* or an *A*? Unfortunately, no. It is only a chronological list of encyclopedia-style facts, not the introduction, development, and conclusion of a real thesis. It is not, in other words, an *essay*. Advanced writing is the perfectly structured presentation of a serious, original idea.

Sarah Connor

English Honors
Mrs. Saranson
May 5, 2008

Emily Dickinson

Born on December 10, 1830, in Amherst, Massachussets, Emily Dickinson would become one of the greatest American poets, even though she was almost completely unknown during her life. Reclusive and taciturn, Dickinson rarely left Amherst, and visited the rest of the world through her imagination:

> Dickinson decked herself in white clothing and rarely left the house. She lived quietly, read Robert Browning's poetry, and took her dog for walks. Any romantic feelings she ever had for anyone came to nothing, and she died unknown and in some ways isolated (Laura Robertson, p. 273).

As a child Dickinson became depressed after a cousin died of typhus. Her emotional condition because serious enough that her parents sent her to Boston to get her out of her environment.

She went to school at Amherst Academy, where she spent seven years studying literature, science, history, mathematics, and Latin. She was ill in 1845 and only attended school for eleven weeks. Her biographer, Ronald Barnes, concluded that Dickinson "attained some of the fundamentals of a true education at Amherst, but not much more than that" (Ronald Barnes, p. 387).

In 1847 Dickinson went to Mount Holyoke Female Seminary, but she only spent ten months there before her brother took her home, and the institution "does not appear to have made a lasting effect on her mind" (Saladin, p. 72). The following year Dickinson busied herself with family and local community life.

Bibliography

Robertson, Laura. (1990) *Emily Dickinson and the Epic Voyage of a Solitary Heart*. New York City: Halfcourt and Bruce Publishing Company.

Barnes, Ronald (2001) *The Evolution of a Major Poet*. Boston: Randel House Inc.

Saladin, Malamud. (1998) *The Genesis Effect: Common Elements in the Lives of Great Creative Minds*. Atlanta: Absalom University Press.

Thomas, Robert. (2007) *Dickinson's Extraordinary Power of Observation*.

Study the differences between these two formats of the same paper very carefully. Our papers will be like the MLA sample on the right.

Sarah Connor

English Honors

Mrs. Saranson

May 5, 2008

Emily Dickinson

Born on December 10, 1830, in Amherst, Massachussets, Emily Dickinson would become one of the greatest American poets, even though she was almost completely unknown during her life. Reclusive and taciturn, Dickinson rarely left Amherst, and she visited the rest of the world through her imagination:

> Dickinson decked herself in white clothing and rarely left the house. She lived quietly, read Robert Browning's poetry, and took her dog for walks. Any romantic feelings she ever had for anyone came to nothing, and she died unknown and in some ways isolated (Laura Robertson, p. 273).

As a child Dickinson became depressed after a cousin died of typhus. Her emotional condition because serious enough that her parents sent her to Boston to get her out of her environment.

She went to school at Amherst Academy, where she spent seven years studying literature, science, history, mathematics, and Latin. She was ill in 1845 and only attended school for eleven weeks. Her biographer, Ronald Barnes, concluded that Dickinson "attained some of the fundamentals of a true education at Amherst, but not much more than that" (Ronald Barnes, p. 387).

In 1847 Dickinson went to Mount Holyoke Female Seminary, but she only spent ten months there before her brother took her home, and the institution "does not appear to have made a lasting effect on her mind" (Saladin, p. 72). The following year Dickinson busied herself with family and local community life.

Bibliography

Robertson, Laura. (1990) *Emily Dickinson and the Epic Voyage of a Solitary Heart*. New York City: Halfcourt and Bruce Publishing Company.

Barnes, Ronald (2001) *The Evolution of a Major Poet*. Boston: Randel House Inc.

Saladin, Malamud. (1998) *The Genesis Effect: Common Elements in the Lives of Great Creative Minds*. Atlanta: Absalom University Press.

Thomas, Robert. (2007) *The Imaginary Concsience of Charles Dickens*

Connor 1

Sarah Connor

Mrs. Saranson

English Honors

5 May 2008

The teacher's name comes second, the course title third.

Emily Dickinson

Born on December 10, 1830, in Amherst, Massachussets, Emily Dickinson would become one of the greatest American poets, even though she was almost completely unknown during her life. Reclusive and taciturn, Dickinson rarely left Amherst, and she visited the rest of the world through her imagination:

> Dickinson decked herself in white clothing and rarely left the house. She lived quietly, read Robert Browning's poetry, and took her dog for walks. Any romantic feelings she ever had for anyone came to nothing, and she died unknown and in some ways isolated. (Robertson 273)

mm As a child, typhus struck Dickinson's cousin, and she became depressed. Her emotional condition because serious enough that her parents sent her to Boston to get her out of her environment.

She went to school at Amherst Academy. Where she spent seven years studying literature, science, history, mathematics, and Latin. She was ill in 1845 and only attended school for eleven weeks. Her biographer, Ronald Barnes, concluded that Dickinson "attained some of the fundamentals of a true education at Amherst, but not much more than that" (Barnes 387). frag

In 1847 Dickinson went to Mount Holyoke Female Seminary, but she only spent ten months there before her brother took her home, and the institution "does not appear to have made a lasting effect on her mind"

Connor 1

Works Cited

Robertson, Laura. Emily Dickinson and the Epic Voyage of a Solitary Heart. New York: Halfcourt, 1990.

Barnes, Ronald. The Evolution of a Major Poet. Boston: Randel, 2001

Saladin, Malamud. (1998) The Genesis Effect: Common Elements in the Lives of Great Creative Minds. Atlanta: Absalom UP, 1998.

Thomas, Robert. Dickinson's Extraordinary Power of Observation. Chicago: U of Epsilon P, 2007.

Once my English and MLA format are right, how do I get a *B*?

So, we get the English right to get a *D*, and we get the MLA format right to get a *C*? Is that standard not too absolute? Should we not receive partial credit if our English is half-right?

No, English is not advanced when only part of it is right. Even the best students sometimes make a few mistakes in a paper, but advanced academic writing does not contain numerous errors per page. Nor will we play a point game, adding errors up and deducting x points per error. This is no game. You either have acceptable English and MLA format or not—these elements are fundamental. The evaluation of a paper is not based on good intentions or on how much someone has improved; it is based on the truth about the paper. One student may have many more things to learn than another in order to reach an acceptable standard; if so, the student must learn them before turning in the paper.

Once your English and MLA format are correct, what do you have to do to get a *B*? You have to organize every sentence and paragraph into a perfect essay structure. You have to leave those one-part encyclopedia-type papers behind, and write true essays: three-part explorations of a thesis, including an introduction, a complex body, and a conclusion. (Every three-part passage is not an essay; the introduction has to introduce a thesis, the body has to develop evidence for it, and the conclusion has to show how all of the evidence means what you say it means.)

Let us look at a sample page of a paper by Woody Feibhur. This is by far the best of the papers we have seen. We see few elementary errors of English, usage, or punctuation. The MLA format is perfect, even including the brackets and ellipsis in the well-chosen quotations to show material inserted and omitted. Finally, here is a paper that a reader can enjoy.

What about the structure? Is this an organized essay, and are the paragraphs and quotations written in a smooth and continuous way? Yes, judging from page one, it is an essay. The first paragraph is a good introduction, informing us that the paper will explore three forms of the call that the dog Buck experiences. The first sentence of each paragraph has words (*of these three forms*, *This call*, *Still*) that gracefully connect the paragraph to the previous one.

This is an accomplished paper. Unfortunately, it has a poor thesis. Woody needed to think more. His thesis is mildly interesting, but we do not learn from it. Anyone knows that the call is a prominent part of this book. For language, format, and structure, we will give Woody a high *B*. For an *A* he needed a stronger thesis.

Feibhur 1

Woody Feibhur

Mrs. Sippie

English

21 May 2008

The Call in London's The Call of the Wild

Jack London's 1903 novel The Call of the Wild is an exciting animal story; the tame dog Buck is gradually lured deep into the fierce wilderness by three experiences: the howl of the wolves, the cruelty of human beings, and by the ferocity of other dogs. These experiences change Buck from an affectionate house dog into a fierce animal, able to live on his own.

The howl of the wolves is the most obvious of these three forms of the call of the wild. It is an audible call that Buck hears. When Buck is with his master John Thornton, he first hears the howl of the wolves:

> Deep in the forest a call was sounding, and as often as he [Buck] heard this call, mysteriously thrilling and luring, he felt compelled to turn his back upon the fire and the beaten earth around it, and to plunge into the forest, and on and on, he knew not where or why; the call sounding imperiously, deep in the forest. (London 57)

This call, the howl of the wolf, is "mysteriously thrilling," "luring," imperious. Buck hears this call at time when he has come to know the wild more deeply than he ever did as a pet at home in the Santa Clara Valley: "Kill or be killed, eat or be eaten, was the law; and this mandate, down out of the depths of Time, he obeyed" (59). Buck understands this mandate, and longs to follow the call, but so long as John Thornton lives, Buck chooses to remain with him. This seems significant because for all its allure, the call of the wild is not the only thing Buck wants and needs; his love for John Thornton and Thornton's love for him mean even more.

Still, the call is strong. Sometimes Buck "pursued the call into the forest, looking for it as though it were a tangible thing" (69), and one night Buck hears the howl of a lean timber wolf: "From the forest came the call . . . distinct and definite as never before--a long-drawn howl, like, any noise made by husky dog" (69).

Feibhur 1

Works Cited

Benson, Frank, and Robert Dulles. The Tenuous and Shifting Relationship between Life and Literature. New York: Halfcourt, 2002

London, Jack. The Call of the Wild. Atlanta: Bignet, 1991.

Philips, Cynthia. The Life of Jack London: How a Seaman Used Great Literature to Ameliorate the Miseries of the Docks. Chicago: Cheetah, 1991.

How do I get an *A*?

To get an *A*, the paper must have good English, good MLA format, good essay structure, and good thinking. What is good thinking? There is no one right way to define it, but we can make a few observations that will help.

It is not an unevaluated summary of the facts or the plot.

The papers we will write require thinking. The student must read, study, research, and think until he or she develops something to say. These papers will not just be well-written plot summaries or chains of encyclopedia facts; the student must have an insight that takes the reader beyond the shallow fact-surface.

It is news; it is original.

We have all had the miserable experience of enduring a long explanation about something that we already understood, something obvious that needed no explanation. That is tedious, and you must not do that to your reader. Present something that the reader does not already know. Too often, the theme of a paper is something that we have heard before, or it is similar to something we have heard before. Some (not all) of the best ideas are startling because they are original, they have a certain ground-breaking quality. They bring an unconventional way of thinking to the problem. An idea could be news but still be only a new variation of ordinary, conventional thinking. Every thesis is not required to be shockingly original.

It matters.

There are some observations that—if they are true—matter. They change the way you view the world, or they change the way you interpret a novel. They are ideas we care about.

Here is a sample paper by Alicia Rivera. It is not a perfect paper; in fact, Alicia will write much better papers later this year. There are a few elementary errors, including a contraction on page two and a run-on sentence and space error on page three. She also broke MLA format by underlining a period in the Works Cited page. The paper does have excellent English, almost perfect MLA format, a clear and connected essay structure, and an interesting idea: the animals in Kenneth Grahame's *The Wind in the Willows* actually admire Toad for the quality that they also believe is his worst fault. Compare this paper to Mike's, Sarah's, and Woody's.

Alicia Rivera

Mr. Roberts

English Honors

21 May 2001

Admiring an Incorrigible Character

In Kenneth Grahame's 1908 classic novel The Wind in the Willows, a poetic story of woodland animals living on the murmuring riverbank, the incorrigible--incapable of correction--character of Toad occupies center stage. Throughout the story Ratty, Mole, and Badger have to contend with the egocentric, unreasonable, and obsessed Toad, as he gets into one jam after another. On the surface of the story, Toad seems to be nothing but trouble for his friends, but in spite of the problems he causes, his animal friends remain loyal to him--liking and even admiring his very frustrating but incorrigible spirit.

Early in the story we learn that Toad has good qualities that the other animals admire; the Mole asks the Rat if he would like to go to Toad Hall and meet Toad:

> "Why, certainly," said the good-natured Rat, jumping to his feet and dismissing poetry from his mind for the day. "Get the boat out, and we'll paddle up there [to Toad Hall] at once. It's never the wrong time to call on Toad. Early or late he's always the same fellow. Always good-tempered, always glad to see you, always sorry when you go!" (Grahame 42)

There are quotation marks in these long quotes only because they are dialogue.

When Mole answers that Toad must be a very nice animal, the Rat elaborates, somewhat equivocally:

> "He is indeed the best of animals . . . So simple, so good-natured, and so affectionate. Perhaps he's not very clever--we can't all be geniuses; and it may be that he is both boastful and conceited. But he has got some great qualities, Toady." (42)

Off they go to Toad Hall to see this "boastful and conceited" fellow with "some great qualities," and they find the best of animals resting in a wicker garden chair. When Toad sees them arrive, he is ecstatic:

"'Hooray!' he cried, jumping up on seeing them, 'this is splendid!'" (43). Toad's good nature does not prevent him, in the ensuing conversation, from boasting about his fine house, from admitting that he has given up on his previous obsession of rowing and boating, and from announcing his new obsession, though Toad himself does not call it an obsession. The incorrigible thinks he has "discovered the real thing, the only genuine occupation for a lifetime" (44).

Toad leads Ratty and Mole out to his coach-house where they see the latest object of Toad's incorrigible passion: a gypsy caravan, "shining with newness, painted a canary-yellow picked out with green, and red wheels" (45). As Ratty and Mole listen, Toad babbles on about his dream of the open road, the dusty highway, and the rolling countryside. Rat whispers to Mole that it will not take Toad very long to get over his interest in this yellow gypsy caravan; it won't last: "His fads never do" (48) the Rat says.

SP

Ratty is right. The very next day, as the animals walk along the roadside, they are nearly run over by Toad's new obsession: a great, speeding, beautiful, loud, new motor-car. At first they hear the motor's sound, poop-poop, in the distance. And then:

> . . . in an instant the peaceful scene was changed, and with a blast of wind and a whirl of sound that made them jump for the nearest ditch, it was on them! The "poop-poop" rang with a brazen shout in their ears, they had a moment's glimpse of an interior of glittering plate-glass and rich morocco, and the magnificent motor-car, immense, breath-snatching, passionate, with its pilot tense and hugging his wheel . . . flung an enveloping cloud of dust that blinded and enwrapped them utterly, and then dwindled to a speck in the far distance, changed back into a droning bee once more. (49-50)

When a long quote begins in the middle of a sentence, we start with an ellipsis (. . .).

So much for gypsy caravans. The impressionable Toad is overwhelmed with enthusiasm for the magnificent motor-car. Suddenly, he wants nothing to do with his "splendid" gypsy cart. # Ratty and Mole see the crazed look in Toad's eye, and Mole asks what they can do. "Nothing at all," the Rat answers: "Because there is really nothing to be done. You see, I know him from of old. He is now possessed" (51).

Ratty is right. When next we see Toad, he too is shouting as he careens out of control around the country roads in his own motor-car. Ratty, Mole, and Badger have to spend the rest of the story trying to save Toad from himself, and in the process they have one grand adventure after another.

In the end we are impressed with the animals' loyal and forgiving spirits. They live by their own code of "animal-etiquette" (33), and they keep their friendships. Toad may be a stubborn and irritating fellow, but Ratty, Mole, and Badger tolerate him and even like him. They go out of their way to visit him. They know he is trouble and lacks self-discipline, but they admire his good nature and friendly disposition. They like his optimism and enthusiasm. Even though Toad is incorrigible and will not listen to their advice, they love his free spirit. It is a lot of work to be Toad's friend, but Ratty, Mole, and Badger do it anyway; Toad is a member of their animal community. This animal decency is an essential lesson in The Wind in the Willows, and is one of the reasons that this book is still meaningful to us, nearly a century after it was written.

R-S

Here is one version of the grading method. Personal, literary, and supportive.

Works Cited

Grahame, Kenneth. The Wind in the Willows. New York: Signet, 1969.

Alicia,

94

I enjoyed your excellent paper on the complex loyalties of Toad's animal friends. There are a few errors to avoid in the future, but this paper is in excellent English and correct MLA format, and it also has a good essay structure. I like the way you tie the paper together with the word incorrigible.

Your thesis is subtle and interesting, and you use quotations well, but I do not think you show enough evidence for the fact that the animals admire Toad's wild (incorrigible) nature. Let me know if you have questions about this.

In your conclusion you should refer more specifically to the evidence you have presented, rather than just summarizing it all in your own words. Tie the threads together for the reader.

Thank you for your close attention to advanced details. I look forward to your next paper.

Key Point Summary

1. Advanced academic writing is not an endless ordeal of having your basic spelling and grammar corrected. You do not even begin to do advanced writing until after you have put basic errors behind you. Advanced academic papers are expected to be completely free of basic mistakes if they are to receive passing grades.

2. Advanced academic papers are not handwritten but are typed according to an advanced format used in high schools and colleges. We will use the Modern Language Association's MLA format, the most widely used format in high schools and colleges. The central point is that when any standard method is assigned, it must be followed to the letter. Quotations that are indented must be indented exactly ten spaces, titles that are centered must be exactly centered, one-inch margins must be one inch. The punctuation and indentation on the Works Cited page must be perfect.

3. Advanced papers are not dashed off like diaries; they are carefully planned and organized before they are written. They include exact quotations from other sources that provide illustration or evidence for a worthwhile thesis. When we do advanced academic writing, we do not write in a hurry. We not only accept but enjoy the relaxed pace of research, the meticulous construction of sentences, the gradual architecture of essays.

4. It is a pleasure to be advanced, just as it is unpleasant not to know what we are doing. The advanced process must be accompanied by an advanced attitude because so long as we resist enjoying advanced competence, we will be unable to achieve it. For important intellectual reasons, the advanced academic writing process must feel like a grown-up form of fun, and we must be excited and relieved that we have an opportunity to learn it now.

Advanced Writing Assignments

This section of the book contains four writing assignments, each more complex and challenging than the former. Each assignment begins with a reflection on vocabulary and grammar. This is followed by a special focus section of ten actual research paper comments emphasizing details of real student papers. Additional components, such as information about outlining, may follow. The specifications of your writing assignments are presented at the end of each section.

FIRST PAPER: ONE SOURCE, INTERPRETATION OF FICTION

Myerors 1

Mark Myerors

Ms. Achussetts

English Honors

10 March 2004

Give less background and put more focus on your thesis.

The Character of a Gift

In Robert Louis Stevenson's classic novel, Kidnapped, an exchange takes place; two characters give to each other in a way that cements their friendship and demonstrates a nobility of character that each one possesses. In no way, shape, or form is this nobility of character trivial; it becomes a central theme of the book, explaining why the main character, David Balfour, is able to survive the challenges that he encounters.

cliché

The scene of the gift begins when David Balfour finds himself on the road in Scotland--hungry, broke, and in need of a friend. Dusty and thirsty, the road stretches on until he sees a man:

mm

> Early in my next day's journey I overtook a little stout, solemn man, walking very slowly with his toes turned out, sometimes reading in a book and sometimes marking the place with his finger, and dressed decently and plainly in something of a clerical style. (Stevenson 107)

This means that the road is thirsty!

tr

The strangers' name is Henderland. Henderland speaks "with the broad south-country [Scottish] tongue" (107), and he is an evangelist in the Edinburgh Society for Propagating Christian Knowledge. As the two walked along, Henderland stops and speaks "with all the wayfarers and workers that we met or passed" (107), and he seems to "be well liked in the countryside" (107).

Henderland is a garrulous conversationalist. He tells David about his work, about the people he knows, and other superfluous information about the region they are traversing. Henderland's affection for people is obvious, and at length he offers David the hospitality of his very own home; he "proposed that I should make a short stage, and lie the night in his house a little beyond [the village of] Kingairloch" (108).

Combine and condense these two paragraphs.

The period comes after the parenthetical in a short quote.

Assignment One: Think like an academic writer — about words.

As you write, think carefully about the words you use. You must use words precisely, and you must choose words that have an academic tone. Write with a dictionary close, and never use a word unless you know its definition and part-of-speech usage.

A rule of thumb is that while you want to use only formal vocabulary in your academic writing, and never contractions or clichés (if these occur in quotations, that is all right), you also do not want to overload your sentences with big words. Good writers often use only one power-word in a sentence, and they do not put them in every sentence. These very strong words are reserved for emphasis, and are often the last word in the sentence because they have more impact there.

One of the ways you learn the tone of academic papers is by absorbing academic vocabulary and getting a feel for how it differs from conversational vocabulary. Here are some formal words from *The Word Within the Word, Volume One,* that are appropriate in a variety of academic papers. Each listing begins with the chapter of *The Word Within the Word* in which it appears:

	Word	Definition	Part of Speech	Example
1.	**superfluous**	excess	adjective	The objection was **superfluous**.
1.	**posthumously**	after death	adverb	The book was published **posthumously**.
2.	**neophyte**	beginner	noun	As a poet, he was a **neophyte**.
2.	**incredulous**	disbelieving	adjective	The readers were **incredulous**.
3.	**specious**	false	adjective	The **specious** argument convinced him.
3.	**elucidate**	explain	verb	Harper Lee **elucidated** the scene.
4.	**equanimity**	calmness	noun	Ahab's **equanimity** was startling.
4.	**magnum opus**	great work	noun	*Walden* was Thoreau's **magnum opus**.
5.	**hyperbole**	overstatement	noun	The claim was mere **hyperbole**.
5.	**altruism**	selflessness	noun	Toad was not known for **altruism**.

Discussion Questions:

Are any of these words completely unknown to you? Which ones? Which word would you most like to add to your vocabulary? Which word might be most useful in formal papers?

Assignment One: Think like an academic writer — about sentences.

Academic writers do not write obliviously, unaware of the construction of their sentences. Instead, there is a grammatical self-awareness that is one of the real pleasures of being a competent writer. After you understand grammar, you know—as you write it—that the sentence is correct, and you enjoy seeing the correct pieces click into place. Reflect on this sentence taken from *4Practice, Volume One*:

His **superflu**ous comments were nothing but a **trans**parent **sub**ter**fuge**.

adj. adj. n. v. pron. conj. adj. adj. n.

Parts of Speech

subj. LVP S.C. --S.C.

Parts of Sentence

----no prepositional, appositive, or verbal phrase----

Phrases

---one independent clause---

a simple declarative sentence

Clauses

Grammar: This sentence is an equation formed by the past tense linking verb *were*. The excitement comes from the beautiful compound subject complement. Notice how different the meaning of *but* is from the meaning of *and*; these are both coordinating conjunctions, but their meanings are almost opposite. The pronoun *nothing* is sometimes referred to as a *negative pronoun*. Note that in this sentence *his* is being used as a possessive adjective rather than a possessive pronoun. The letters LVP mean Linking Verb Predicate. When you see AVP, that means Action Verb Predicate.

When we write a sentence, we combine all elements of language together.

Vocabulary: The adjective *superfluous* means more than enough; *super* means over, and *flu* means flow. The noun *subterfuge* refers to a form of deceitful ducking of a question or issue; *sub* means under, and *fug* means flee. The stem *trans* means across. W1 (W1 means that the bold stems are from *The Word Within the Word*, *Volume One*, List 1.)

Poetics: The sentence ends in powerful iambics: trans PAR / ent SUB / ter FUGE.

Writing: We see the power word *subterfuge* placed last, for maximum effect.

Punctuation: There is no comma before the conjunction; it does not join two clauses.

Students could study this page as homework, to be followed by a short quiz at the beginning of class.

Assignment One: Focus Areas — Actual Research Paper Comments

You cannot focus on hundreds of things at once. Each of the four assignments in this text emphasizes ten important writing details. They may be details of grammar, style, format, or thought. These comments are drawn from my decades of assigning and grading advanced academic writing in the classroom; they are specimens, word-for-word comments that I actually did write on students' papers. Some of them are re-examinations of points we have already seen. Some of them are big ideas, and some of them involve little perfections (small details are not unimportant; that is one of the major realizations of academic writing). These comments show common issues for students who are just learning to write advanced academic papers.

Here are three positive comments:

1. A discussion of ideas, not just a report.
One of the advanced features of your paper is that the paper is not a mere report; it is a display of your reasoning. You do not limit yourself to the role of reporter, humbly displaying other people's statements; instead, you structure your paper as an argument, a display of your own ideas in which you use facts and expert comment to support what you say. That is excellent.

2. Good proofreading.
One of the best features of your work is the excellent proofreading you have done. This makes your paper free of the irritating elementary errors that distract a reader's attention away from ideas. Advanced polish and detail like this makes your paper pleasant to read; it brings your thoughts to the fore.

3. Well-chosen quotations.
A quality that distinguishes your paper is your excellent selection of material for quotation. These well-chosen quotations lend force and cogency to your argument. They also provide the reader with extremely interesting passages to read, and they show a high level of comprehension on your part.

Rivera 3

to do with his "splendid" gypsy cart. Ratty and Mole see the crazed look in Toad's eye, and Mole asks what they can do. "Nothing at all," the Rat answers: "Because there is really nothing to be done. You see, I know him from of old. He is now possessed." (51) ... see Toad, he too is shouting as he

Here are comments about areas that need improvement:

4. Use proper paragraphs. ¶
Use proper paragraphs. The paragraph symbol ¶ means that you should have indented five spaces to start the next paragraph. Be sure to paragraph your work properly. Usually, begin a new paragraph after a long quotation.

5. Your conclusion is listy.
Your conclusion contains many good things, but they are not organized well, separated clearly, tied together revealingly, or expressed surprisingly. It reads like a list of repetitions of things you said before. I want you to concentrate on the art of writing a convincing conclusion that will impress, interest, inform, and convince a reader.

6. Your conclusion is undeveloped.
Please write a carefully developed conclusion. Now that you have shown the reader all of the evidence for your thesis, it is time to show what the evidence means; you cannot expect the reader to remember everything and total it all up for himself. You cannot expect the reader to draw the conclusions; you have to do it. Review the most important ideas, but do not just repeat the headlines from the body. Do not just go back over things you have already said. In the conclusion, go to a new height. Take the time to pull themes together, to highlight relationships, and to synthesize all of the information into a final recognition. Do not introduce new themes, but show the implications and the interrelations of the various ideas previously explored in your paper. Remember that the conclusion is your first real chance to discuss everything because it is not until the conclusion that the reader has finally been presented with all of the facts and ideas that appeared in the body.

7. Clarify your paragraphs' relationships.
At times in your paper I had difficulty understanding how what I was reading related to what I had just read. The reader needs to know the logical status of each paragraph. Is it another example supporting what was said in the previous paragraph? Is this a contrasting idea? Have we begun a completely new section of the paper? How, exactly, does this idea relate to the thesis? In beginning each paragraph, you need to write something that will show the reader the relationship of this paragraph to the previous paragraph and to the thesis. Like an essay, a paragraph needs an introduction, even if it only consists of a few connecting words, such as "Another reason that Euripides was condemned by Aristophanes was . . . " You might even need an entire connecting paragraph just to clarify the relationship between the previous several paragraphs and the following several paragraphs.

8. You have a sentence fragment. (frag)

Please write in complete sentences, avoiding sentence fragments. My proofreader's mark frag indicates the presence in your paper of a sentence fragment, one of the most serious grammar errors. It is essential, in a formal research paper, to write in complete sentences. There must be a subject, a predicate, and a complete thought in every sentence you write. Common types of sentence fragments include: 1) Dependent clauses punctuated as though they were sentences: "When Melville went to sea. His real adventure had begun." 2) Participial phrases punctuated as though they were sentences: "After deserting the ship. Melville lived among cannibals." 3) Verbless subject and appositive clusters: "Herman Melville, a seafaring author." 4) Subjectless predicates: "Melville arrived. Went to the Inn." 5) Groups of confused words: "Melville in the seafaring adventure cannibals." 6) Fragments caused by using quotations in a way that fails to complete the thought: "Spencer believed that social struggle 'for existence as leading to the perfect society.'" 7) The "being" fragment, in which you mistake the word "being" for a verb: "Dante described nine circles of the Inferno. The first circle being Limbo."

9. Your thesis word is misspelled. (sp)

Spell your key words correctly! A surprisingly common and embarrassing error is to misspell the key word of the paper. An example would be to misspell Shakespear in a paper about Shakespeare, to spell Iliad Illiad, to write a paper about Thoreau's Walden and spell it Waldon, or to write a paper about Jonathan Swift and spell his name Jonathon.

10. You have a misplaced modifier. (mm)

Avoid misplaced modifiers. My mm mark means that you have a misplaced modifier, a serious error in grammar. You must develop a sense of modifier placement. Words, phrases, and even clauses that act as modifiers must be placed next to or as close as possible to the things they modify. If you put the modifier somewhere else, it will modify something else, and the result is often nonsense. Some examples: If you say that "In an effort to be modest, Whitman's first edition of poetry lacked his name," that means that the book was being modest--a ridiculous idea. To correct the modification error, place the modifier next to the word you really intend to modify: "In an effort to be modest, Whitman omitted his name from the first edition of his poetry." The sentence, "An idealist, most of Plato's ideas are only ideals" means that ideas are idealists! Better would have been, "An idealist, Plato regarded his ideas as ideals." "Feeling alone and desperate, this was one of Dinesen's last letters" means that a letter felt desperate. Correct would have been, "Feeling alone and desperate, Dinesen wrote one of her last letters." Modifiers are like lights; they illuminate things close to them, and so you have to put them next to their intended targets.

Have students choose and defend the problem they think is most important.

Assignment One: Organization and Outline.

You must outline your paper before you write it.

Your teacher might require you to write a formal outline and turn it in, although for such a short paper as this one that is often not necessary. Formally or informally, organize your thinking until you know exactly what you are going to do. If you are asked for a formal outline, it will help you to examine this example from my *Essay Voyage* text. Many computer word processors have this outline format as a built-in option.

```
Thesis: Invisible Forces Hold the Universe Together

 I.     Introduction.
        A.  There are four known forces of nature.
            1.  The forces are invisible but powerful.
            2.  Each force acts in a different way.
            3.  More than one force affects every object.
II.     Body.
        A.  Gravitation
            1.  Gravitation is the weakest force.
            2.  Gravitation has infinite range.
            3.  Its force is based on mass.
            4.  It works on all objects in the universe.
        B.  Electromagnetism
            1.  Electromagnetism acts between charged particles.
            2.  It is much stronger than gravitation.
            3.  It also has infinite range.
        C.  The Strong Force
            1.  It holds the nuclei of atoms together.
            2.  It binds quarks together in clusters.
        D.  The Weak Force
            1.  The sun would not burn without it.
            2.  It is responsible for radioactivity.
            3.  It governs the decay of subatomic particles.
III.    Conclusion.
        A.  Four invisible forces hold the universe together.
            1.  If the forces suddenly stopped:
                a. All stars, planets, and moons would fly out of orbit.
                b. All electricity would stop.
                c. All atoms would fly apart.
                d. All subatomic particles would fly apart.
            2.  This would not be good.
            3.  They have not stopped; there is no recorded exception.
        B.  Human beings have mass and electrical charge, and they are
            made of atoms, so the four forces preserve us.
```

It is the research that gradually generates the details of the outline.

Assignment One: Planning and Preparing the First Paper.

As you begin, keep in mind that you have a choice: you can be either happy or unhappy when you have formal writing assignments. You have to do such assignments either way, so you may as well enjoy learning something important and try to select subjects that you would love to know about. Academic happiness is a sign of intellectual maturity. Follow these five steps:

1. Read, reread, take notes, think. Repeat as necessary.

You begin, always, by reading books. As we have seen, academic papers are not about nothing, and they are also not expressions of our personal feelings or preferences. They are not unsupported opinions. They are about academic truth: interpretations of important novels, examinations of scientific ideas, considerations of historical hypotheses. So you get to read—to find something worth saying about the subject—and you always spend more time reading, thinking, and taking notes than you do writing. This is one of the reasons academic papers are so important in our intellectual development: they push us into deep investigations.

One of the fatal mistakes beginners make is to be impatient about the reading-thinking stage. If you attempt to write too soon, if you do not settle down for a good read, you are in trouble because good ideas are not on the surface to be scooped up by skimmers. The good ideas are down in the crevices of the story, hidden in the nuances, waiting in the shadows where serious and respectful readers can find them. You have to read enough to write enough.

The most common reason that students are impatient with reading and research is that they have negative attitudes or feelings about reading. It is essential that you think and feel positively, that you define yourself as someone who loves to read and learn, and that you believe in the value and meaning of your topic. Great academic minds are always believers, excited about knowledge; without that excitement, they would never push themselves to high achievements. You work on what you care about.

Your teacher will give you specific guidelines about the literature selections you may use, and it will then be up to you to read, slowly and carefully, and reread (research shows that the best readers re-read and re-re-read), searching for an interesting observation. Once you notice something good, then you will reread yet again to find lines in the text that you can quote to support and illustrate your case.

What kind of idea would be interesting? It should be something that is not obvious to everyone who reads the book. No one wants to read a case that Captain Hook is a villain. We all know that. Your thesis should be a *contribution* to the existing knowledge. It should require a new case to be made, and your paper is the case.

2. Organize and Outline.

As you read, you begin to see how to organize your paper. You find good quotations that support your argument. Your teacher may or may not require you to turn in an outline, but formally or informally, outline your paper. Plan your introduction, body, and conclusion. Decide what quotations to use and where to put them. Know your plan well before you start writing.

3. Write your first, high-quality draft.

Do not write what is sometimes called a *rough draft*; even a first draft should be carefully written—not rough. If your first version is rough, it will take you twice as long to write the paper because you will have made a mess to clean up. From the beginning, write carefully, as though you knew you would not be able to revise. Write the essay in sections: introduction, body, and conclusion. Use a key thesis word consistently to tie the sections together. Write clear transitions between paragraphs. Write a patient, thoughtful, and complete conclusion. Doing your first draft on a computer makes revision much easier later.

4. Take a break, then revise.

Get away from the essay until your mind clears and you can see what you have actually written. Once you can be objective, revise the paper carefully. Almost certainly, the first draft will be too wordy, and you will be removing unnecessary words, or sentences, or even paragraphs.

5. Proofread.

Proofreading takes a long time. Check each detail, over and over. It is impossible to proofread rapidly. You have to go very slowly, checking each word and punctuation mark, each MLA detail. Advanced academic proofreading requires a tough, disciplined mind.

Assignment One • Interpretation of Fiction

Advanced Academic Details

This first essay will give you an opportunity to fine-tune your details. Remember that this is one of the first expectations of advanced academic writing: the basic details of language, format, and essay form must be correct. Let us look at a summary of the assignment:

Purpose: Establishing a Basic Foundation

This simple essay using only one book will give you an opportunity to concentrate on the basic details of English, MLA, and essay format.

Topic: Interpretation of a Classic Work of Fiction

Your essay will develop an interpretive idea about a work of fiction. You may not a write a biographical paper about the author's life. The work may be a novel, play, or even short story, depending upon your teacher's instruction. Your interpretive idea will be the thesis of your essay. It need not be a Nobel Prize grand idea; a focused but illuminating observation about the facts or meaning of the story will be appropriate to the short length of the paper. You need not write about the main theme of the work if you do not wish to; you may choose something smaller that you notice and wish to write about. Your teacher may provide additional specifications or limitations on the topic.

Length: Three pages

This paper must be no more than three pages long, with a fourth page for the Works Cited. Page three should contain a half-page or more of text.

Due Date: Your teacher will assign the date, providing at least two weeks for both research and writing. Late papers will lose one letter grade per day.

Format: MLA

This will be an MLA essay with long and short quotations. A paper done in any other format will be returned to the student to be redone. The teacher may assign a letter-grade-per-day penalty for lateness in such a case. The paper should be typed on one side of the page only, in ragged-right, double-spaced Courier type font, ten- or twelve-point size. There must be a minimum of one long quotation and three short quotations in the paper.

Structure: Essay

This paper should be a three-part thesis essay, with introduction, body, and conclusion. The paragraphs should be organized and clearly connected. Use a key word from your thesis to connect the paper.

Source: One Source Required

For this first paper only one source is required: the text of fiction itself. You may base your analysis entirely on your own thinking, using quotations from the work of fiction to illustrate and prove your idea.

Honor: Your Plagiarism Pledge

Before you turn your paper in, you should write on page four, "I know that plagiarism is the unacknowledged use of someone else's words or ideas, and I pledge that this paper is not plagiarized" and sign it. A plagiarized paper will receive a zero.

Here is a sample paper that—if I were grading it in our imaginary class—would make an *A* on this assignment. Read and examine it very closely. In my actual high school and middle school advanced academic classes, I would have given it:

1. A D, because it is in good English.
2. A C, because it is in proper MLA form.
3. A B, because it is a correct essay structure.
4. An A, because it has an interesting, worthwhile idea.

The word detail is repeated in order to tie the essay together. It provides continuity.

Erchiff 1

Hank Erchiff

Mr. Markemoff

English Honors

18 April 2006

The Power of Detail in Treasure Island

Robert Louis Stevenson's children's classic, Treasure Island, is a story of high adventure in which a young boy, Jim Hawkins, sets sail for buried treasure, only to find himself in the clutches of a band of pirates, led by the crafty Long John Silver. The story has a rich plot that stirs our imaginations, but Stevenson's greatest achievement may be the perfectly chosen details that bring his characters to life. Stevenson assembles these perfect details into a kind of detail-language that we can understand, in order to interpret his characters' motivations correctly.

On the first page of the novel an old seaman--we later learn that his name is Billy Bones--trudges up to the Admiral Benbow Inn, owned by young Jim Hawkins's father. Jim Hawkins recalls:

> I remember him as if it were yesterday, as he came plodding to the inn door, his sea-chest following behind him in a hand-barrow--a tall, strong, heavy, nut-brown man, his tarry pigtail falling over the shoulders of his soiled blue coat, his hands ragged and scarred, with black, broken nails, and the sabre cut across one cheek, a dirty, livid white. (Stevenson 11)

This paragraph discusses the quotation above it, using words from the quotation.

The secrets of that description are in the details. The seaman is nut-brown from sailing, and he can put all of his worldly possessions in a sea-chest. His hands are ragged and his fingernails are broken and black as a result of hard work aboard ship and of a life devoid of personal grooming. Even more revealing, he has a huge scar on his face, and Jim knows at sight that it is a sabre cut which, by the dirty and livid look of it, did not receive proper medical attention; the man's past is evidently disreputable. Stevenson provides all of this information on the first page of the story--in one sentence.

Billy Bones looks like the seaworn pirate he is, but Stevenson used the opposite strategy for the details of Long John Silver, who is a cunning, intelligent villain, deceptive both in intent and in appearance. So clever is Silver that even after Jim Hawkins is warned to beware of a seafaring man with one leg, he trusts Silver anyway. Hawkins first spies Silver at the Spy-glass Inn, where:

> . . . a man came out a side room, and at a glance I was sure he must be Long John. His left leg was cut off close by the hip, and under the left shoulder he carried a crutch, which he managed with wonderful dexterity, hopping about upon it like a bird. He was very tall and strong, with a face as big as a ham--plain and pale, but intelligent and smiling. Indeed, he seemed in the most cheerful spirits, whistling as he moved about among the tables, with a merry word or a slap on the shoulder for the more favored of his guests. (54)

Once again, the details are telling. There is a contradiction between Silver's missing leg and crutch and his quick motions, sharp mind, and fixed smile. Long John Silver's amiable manner will prove to be a malicious facade, and in this first encounter we can see qualities that will make him a fearsome enemy: his surprising physical quickness, his intelligence, and his specious smile. The credulous Jim Hawkins is fooled by Silver's smile; Hawkins observes that he at first worried that this would be the evil one-legged pirate the old seaman at the Admiral Benbow Inn had warned him about, but that "one look at the man before me was enough. I had seen the captain, and Black Dog, and the blind man, Pew, and I thought I knew what a buccaneer was like--a very different creature, according to me, from this clean and pleasant-tempered landlord" (54).

Stevenson's use of detail is focused. He does not assemble descriptions randomly or completely; instead, he ignores distracting or irrelevant details and focuses on details that express the core of the character or the plot. When Jim Hawkins comes upon Ben Gunn, who had been marooned on Treasure Island for three years, Jim is startled by Gunn's appearance; Stevenson focuses on details of clothing:

> Of all the beggar-men that I had seen . . . he was the chief for raggedness. He was clothed with tatters of old ship's canvas and old sea-cloth, and this extraordinary patchwork was all held together by a system of the most various and incongruous fastenings, brass buttons, bits of stick, and loops of tarry gaskin. About his waist he wore an old brass-buckled leather belt, which was the one solid thing in his whole accoutrement. (93)

What Gunn is wearing, in the strict sense, is not clothing at all, because he has been marooned on the island so long that his real clothing fell to pieces. He has garbed himself in scraps of canvas sail, strung together not with any one thing but with a collection of creative connections, indicating the poverty of resources he has had at his disposal in his lonely years on the island. As he speaks to Jim, he stares at Jim's clothes: "All this time [Ben Gunn] had been feeling the stuff of my jacket . . . looking at my boots" (94). By focusing closely on these details of clothing, Stevenson tells us volumes about the life Gunn has had to lead.

The details of description that Stevenson used for Billy Bones, John Silver, and Ben Gunn have imnportant literary characteristics in common. As a group, these three descriptions are not general visual surveys of the characters. They are not, as Jim promises at the beginning of his story, "the whole particulars" (11) rather, they are deliberate close-ups of particular features, chosen to elucidate the characters' lives and motivations. From these perfectly worded descriptions, we can infer the depth of Billy Bones's rough past, the insidious menace of Long John Silver, and the desperate privation of Ben Gunn's lonely years on Treasure Island. Stevenson focuses on these critical details, avoiding the temptation to add other less important facts that would distract our attention. By providing this sharp focus on details, Stevenson helps us understand the story of Jim Hawkins's adventure on Treasure Island.

The conclusion mentions each section of the body and shows how they fit together into meaning.

Works Cited

Stevenson, Robert Louis. <u>Treasure Island</u>. New York: Signet, 1981.

I know that plagiarism is the unacknowledged use of someone else's words or ideas, and I pledge that this paper is not plagiarized.

Hank Erchiff

SECOND PAPER: MULTIPLE WORKS CITED

Menn 1

Mary Menn

Mrs. Askalott

English Honors

24 February 2007

The Character of Neverland

Is Peter Pan the story of Peter Pan? Scholars of British literature are not unanimous in selecting Peter as the main character of James M. Barrie's children's classic, Peter Pan. In fact, three prominent interpretations--by Angus Biph, Fran Chahfriee, and Sal Addgreen--appear to contradict each other, arguing that the hero of the story is Peter, Tinkerbell, and the crocodile, respectively. A close reading of Peter Pan suggests that these seeming disagreements can be resolved, if we view Neverland itself as a main character.

Angus Biph, a professor of literature at Addle University and the author of Crocodiles Can't Tell Time, argues that "Peter is obviously the protagonist of Peter Pan. He is who the other characters have in common, and everything rotates around him" (Biff 87). Biph explains that:

> Peter is the magnetic center of the story. All eyes are on him. Tink loves him; the lost boys follow him; Captain Hook hates him; Wendy and her brothers accompany him, and the crocodile wants to eat him. No other character in Neverland has that clout. Even Hook, for all his arrogance, is jealous. (146)

The first sentence of this paragraph bridges back to the quotation.

Biph's view of Peter does not persuade Fran Chafriee. In Tinkerbell's Secret Plot, a biographical account of Barrie's life, Chafriee says that interpretations "by Biph and others miss the point. Peter carries on in his boyish way, oblivious to all around him, while Tinkerbell operates behind the scenes to keep him safe" (Chafrye 49). In Chafriee's view it is "Tinkerbell's devotion to Peter and her tireless [...]een guard that are responsible for saving not only Peter but [...] She says that "Tinkerbell is the [...]kling provide

Works Cited Menn 4

Addgreen, Sal. Tick, Croc: Why Barrie Designed a Story about a Clock-Eating Crocodile. New York: Halfcourt, 1998.

Barrie, James M. Peter Pan. Atlanta: Bignet, 2008.

Biph, Angus. Crocodiles Can't Tell Time, Chicago: Addle UP, 2001.

Chahfrye, Fran. Tinkerbell's Secret Plot. Los Angel[...]

1995

Assignment Two: Think like an academic writer — about words.

Continue to think about words, not only their definitions, but how they work. If you want to build a strong vocabulary, you must understand the use of nouns, adjectives, and verbs.

As a writer, you cannot be vague about these parts of speech. You must understand the grammar of vocabulary in order to use it with power. Trying to use words means understanding their definitions precisely and understanding the part of speech of the word. The parts of speech are the instructions for vocabulary. For example, if you do not understand your basic grammar, you might write something like: "Charles Dickens settled into a sinecure job"; the problem with that is that *sinecure* is not an adjective, it is a noun.

Formal academic words have a different tone from colloquial words, so it helps to see lots of examples of them. Here are more formal words from *The Word Within the Word, Volume One,* that are appropriate in a variety of academic papers. Each listing begins with the chapter of *The Word Within the Word* in which it appears:

	Word	Definition	Part of Speech	Example
6.	**egregious**	shocking	adjective	It was an **egregious** offense.
6.	**preclude**	prevent	verb	His statement **precluded** any resolution.
7.	**egocentric**	self-centered	adjective	It is **egocentric** poetry.
7.	**exculpate**	exonerate	verb	Her alibi **exculpated** her from blame.
8.	**supersede**	replace	verb	The interpretation **superseded** all others.
8.	**vociferous**	loud	adjective	Long John was a **vociferous** villain.
9.	**platitude**	a trite remark	noun	The essay is full of hollow **platitudes**.
9.	**colloquial**	conversational	adjective	The text was **colloquial**, not formal.
10.	**discursive**	rambling	adjective	The essay was not **discursive**, it was focused.
10.	**pedestrian**	inferior	adjective	We soon tired of his **pedestrian** babble.

Discussion Questions

Which of these words do you think is most powerful? Which word would you least like to be called? Which word might be common in novels? Which word might be found in a book of history?

Assignment Two: Think like an academic writer — about sentences.

Academic writers do not write obliviously, unaware of the construction of their sentences. Instead, there is a grammatical self-awareness that is one of the real pleasures of being a competent writer. After you understand grammar, you know—as you write it—that the sentence is correct, and you enjoy seeing the correct pieces click into place. Reflect on this sentence taken from *4Practice, Volume One*:

	The	**loqu**acious	Spartacus	gave	his	gladiator-army	hope	of	freedom.
Parts of Speech	adj.	adj.	n.	v.	adj.	n.	n.	prep.	n.
Parts of Sentence			subj.	AVP		I.O.	D.O.		
Phrases								----prep. phrase----	
Clauses	----one independent clause----								
	a simple declarative sentence								

Grammar: Notice the indirect object; when we have an I.O., it will always be between the AVP and the D.O.

Vocabulary: The adjective *loquacious* means talkative; *loqu* means talk, and *ous* means full of. Knowing grammar is the key to using vocabulary. You cannot say, "I'm a loquacious" because as this sentence illustrates, *loquacious* is an adjective.

Poetics: By alliterating *final freedom*, just as Lincoln did with *new nation*, we increase the attention that the noun *freedom* receives. On the other hand, the sentence ends weakly on an unstressed syllable; would it be a better sentence if it were rewritten so that the last word was *free*?

Writing: Editing is really only a fancy word for thinking. Q: Put this sentence to an editing test: can you find a word that, if we removed it, would make the sentence stronger?

Punctuation: The hyphen glues *gladiator* and *army* together into a single noun.

Students could study this page as homework, to be followed by a short quiz at the beginning of class.

Assignment Two: Focus Areas — Actual Research Paper Comments

Here are more comments that focus on areas of potential difficulty. Keep in mind that these comments are archived from decades of grading actual student papers; they are things that I had to say to students again and again. If you can internalize these details, then you may not have to learn them the hard way. We saw ten comments in the first assignment; here are ten more. When you write your second paper, continue to focus on the first ten comments, but take these to heart as well.

1. Your MLA details are excellent
I really appreciate the excellent job you have done of following the MLA format. Your first page, your documentary technique, your margins and spacing, and your Works Cited listings all show advanced attention to detail. This gives me, as a reader, more time to spend thinking about your ideas.

2. Good clause punctuation
You have done a good job punctuating the clauses in your sentences. I do not see any run-on sentences or comma splices in the paper. Attention to clauses makes a big difference in how clear and understandable your paper is.

3. Connect the sections of your essay.
When you write the paragraphs and sections of your paper, you must write connecting sentences and phrases--usually at the beginning of each new paragraph or section--which show the reader that you have left the previous idea behind and that you are now moving to a different idea that is related to the previous idea in a specific way. You have to write both the sections and the connections. Otherwise, the paper is like the pieces of a model that have not yet been glued together.

4. You have a pronoun case error (pron)
It is important to apply the rule for pronoun case: a subject is a subject and an object is an object. In other words, the clause subject and the subject complement both take subject pronouns, but the direct object, indirect object, and object of preposition must all take object pronouns. Alexander felt a rivalry between HIM and his father, NOT between HE and his father--the object of preposition must use an object pronoun.

5. The proofreading is terrible.

I am sorry to have to emphasize that this paper shows a serious lack of editing and proofreading. You simply have not taken the time to perfect the details of spelling, punctuation, or grammar. You must understand that proofreading is not a brief concluding activity; it is a methodical, detailed, time-consuming, professional process in which you completely rid your paper of elementary errors. You will have to change your proofreading methods if you are to write polished and advanced papers. Whatever method you are presently using to make sure that your paper is ready to turn in, stop doing that, and do something different.

6. You have a subject/verb disagreement (s/v)

Always make your verbs agree with your subjects. My mark s/v indicates subject/verb disagreement, one of the most serious and embarrassing errors of grammar. Remember that your verb must always agree with, and ONLY WITH, the subject of the sentence--no matter what else comes between the subject and the verb, such as intervening adverbs and prepositional phrases that make you forget what subject you are matching your verb to. Also remember that certain pronouns are always singular, such as <u>each</u>, <u>someone</u>, <u>somebody</u>, <u>everyone</u>, and <u>everybody</u>. Notice the subject/verb disagreement in the following sentence: "Each of his stories contain some philosophical view." Each/contain should be corrected to Each/contains.

7. A special subject/verb problem: the OP Trap

Your paper indicates that you need to review the rule: do not match your verb to the object of a preposition! See the disagreement in the following sentence: "Dostoevsky's views on ethics is best summed up . . ." The intervening prepositional phrase <u>on ethics</u> distracts your mind from the real subject of the sentence, <u>views</u>, and you wind up saying views/is rather than views/are. We see the same problem in this sentence: "The tone of Aristotle's writings were different." Tone/was, not tone/were. The subject is not <u>writings</u>, it is <u>tone</u>. Or: "The impact of Plato's ideas are present in the world today." Impact/is. Or: "Two of the major themes in <u>Don Quixote</u> was humor and irony." Two/were. Or: "The popularity of Pasternak's political struggles have overshadowed the quality of his novel." Popularity/has. Beware of intervening material, especially prepositional phrases; the subject must agree with the verb. Always find the real subject as you write your verb.

Notice that if the subject and verb do not agree, then your sentence is contradicting itself, because one is indicating that the idea is about something singular, while the other is indicating that the idea is about something plural. This means that the fundamental idea of your sentence is nonsense!

8. You have spelling errors. (sp)

One unacceptable problem in your paper, as you see, is that you have numerous spelling errors, which are not acceptable at this mature level of academic work. It is your responsibility to use a dictionary until every word in your paper is spelled correctly. Do not be lazy about using a dictionary; if you think a word is probably spelled correctly, you can be sure that it is not. I have placed the sp proofreader's mark beside spelling errors. Please do whatever you must to rid your papers of spelling errors in the future.

9. Please transpose these elements. (tr)

My tr mark means that you have words or letters that are out of order and that need to be transposed back into the order in which they belong. I would place a tr mark beside misspellings such as thier or beside awkward constructions such as "Then became he indignant." I would also do this if you wrote "Alighieri Dante" because Dante is the first name, and Alighiere is the last name.

10. Avoid exaggeration.

Beware of exaggerated claims and unsupported generalities. If you claim that "no other author has ever" done something, what is your evidence? Are you prepared to discuss the work of every other author and demonstrate its inadequacy? The "most people" error also falls in this category. If you claim that most people think x, do you have evidence in the form of polls or statistics or even quotations from social science that a majority of people think x, or are you just exaggerating? In a formal paper you do not guess or exaggerate; your statements are expected to be the truth; accurate and defensible just as they are expressed.

The header must NOT contain a comma.

Menn 1

Mary Menn

Mrs. Askalott

English Honors

24 February 2007

The Character of Neverland

Is Peter Pan the story of Peter Pan? Scolars of British literature are not unanimous in selecting Peter as the main character of James M. Barrie's children's classic, Peter Pan. In fact, three prominent interpretations--by Angus Biph, Fran Chahfriee, and Sal Addgreen--appears to contradict one another, arguing that the hero the of story is Peter, Tinkerbell, and the crocodile, respectively. A close reading of Peter Pan suggests that these seeming disagreements can be resolved, if we view Neverland itself as the main character.

Angus Biph, a professor of ...

Assignment Two • Works Cited Variations

So far we have used the simplest Works Cited option as our model: a book by a single author. Assignment Two may lead you to different kinds of sources, such as books by multiple authors, more than one book by the same author, introductions, and articles in journals. For instructions on dozens of possible kinds of sources you will want to look at the *MLA Handbook*, but most of our sources will be from these kinds:

A book by multiple authors.

When you cite a book by multiple authors, list them in the same order as they appear in the title page of the book, and give first name first after the first author.

Johnson 4

Works Cited

Jones, Mark, and Robert Adams. Thirteen Ways of Looking at Wallace Stevens's Poetry. Chicago: Bartrum, 2001.

Multiple books by the same author.

On your Works Cited page, if you use more than one book by the same author, do not list out the full name each time. Alphabetize the listings by the same author by their titles, but instead of retyping the author's name each time, type three hyphens.

Johnson 4

Works Cited

Hargrave, Michelle. Emerson, Poe, and the Politics of Poetics. New York: Bignet, 2007.

---. Thomas Hardy and His Critics: A Story of Literary Discouragement. Des Moines: Randle, 2002.

---. Xenophon and the Anabasis. Chicago: U of Martin P, 1998.

An Introduction (or Preface or Foreword).

Often, you can find outstanding commentary in the introduction to a classic novel; typically, the introduction is written by a specialist in the literature of the era, or by a specialist on that particular author. If you wish to cite such a comment, list it by the name of the person who wrote the introduction, and give the name of the author after the title.

Johnson 4

Works Cited

Gregson, Susan. Introduction. Treasure Island. By Robert Louis Stevenson. Chicago: Bartrum, 2001.

Riddle, George. Foreword. Great Expectations. By Charles Dickens. New York: Randle, 1992.

An Article in a Periodical.

Periodicals are journals that appear periodically. Such a journal might appear quarterly and have five or six articles devoted to a particular field of study. If you wish to cite a periodical, use the author's name first, the title of the article in quotation marks, the title of the journal underlined, the volume number, date, and the page numbers of the article. Punctuate and space it this way:

Johnson 4

Works Cited

Gregson, Susan. "The Odyssey of Jim Hawkins." The Stevenson Quarterly Review. 2 (2008): 27-32.

The period after a title must not be underlined.

Menn 4

Works Cited

Addgreen, Sal. Tick, Croc: Why Barrie Designed a Story about a Clock-Eating Crocodile. New York: Halfcourt, 1998.

Biph, Angus. Crocodiles Can't Tell Time. Chicago: Addle UP, 2001.

Chahfrye, Fran. Tinkerbell's Secret Plot. Los Angeles: U of Absalom P, 1995.

Gregson, Susan. "The Odyssey of Jim Hawkins." The Stevenson Quarterly Review. 2 (2008): 27-32.

Hargrave, Michelle. Emerson, Poe, and the Politics of Poetics. New York: Bignet, 2007.

---. Thomas Hardy and His Critics: A Story of Literary Discourse.

Des Moines: Randle, 200[illegible]

Assignment Two • Multiple Works Cited

Purpose: Extracting the Essence of an Idea from Library Research

In the electronic age of computers, video games, and the internet, it is more than ever important to pursue the excitement of real reading. Your academic future will depend in part upon your technological savvy, but you will be surprised how profoundly—in high school, college, and graduate school—you will need to use the library. This assignment will send you to the library and to books and journals on paper. Your goal is to become a library detective, able to find whatever you need to find. This takes experience, and experience takes time.

This assignment brings to focus the word *research*. The reason research is called *research* is that you have to search and then *re*search—search again. Good researchers keep thinking of more ways to look something up.

Topic: A Topic Incorporating Multiple Sources

For the first assignment you had to read a single text thoughtfully, searching for a worthwhile insight to explain and document. This assignment is different; now you will need to read a number of texts about the same topic, searching for a unifying concept you can explain and document. The idea of this paper is, in a sense, between the books.

The first paper had to be about a work of fiction. This paper does not have that restriction, but it is limited to a strong academic topic. You cannot, for example, research a pop music group or a trendy author of light science fiction. The topic must be seriously educational, leaving you with real knowledge that you did not have before. You might, for example, learn what several scholars think about the effect Lewis Carroll's life had on his story, *Alice in Wonderland*. Make it easy on yourself; the more classic something is, the more material is in the library.

Most of the specifications for this paper remain unchanged; the main difference is in the topic and in the sources required. Your teacher will provide you with additional guidelines that connect the assignment to your existing coursework.

Length: **Three pages**

This paper must be no more than three pages long, with a fourth page for the Works Cited. Page three should not be almost blank; it should contain a half-page or more of text.

Due Date: Your teacher will assign the due date, providing at least two weeks for both research and writing. Late papers will lose one letter grade per day.

Format: **MLA**

This will be an MLA essay with long and short quotations. A paper done in any other format will be returned to the student to be redone. The teacher may assign a letter-grade-per-day penalty for lateness in such a case. The paper should be typed on one side of the page only, in ragged-right, double-spaced Courier type font, ten or twelve point size. There must be a minimum of one long quotation and three short quotations in the paper.

Structure: **Essay**

This paper should be a three-part thesis essay, with introduction, body, and conclusion. The paragraphs should be organized and clearly connected. Use a key word from your thesis to connect the paper.

Source: **Four Sources Required**

For this second paper at least four sources must be listed in your Works Cited page. Each must be quoted or cited somewhere in your paper. No elementary encyclopedias, popular magazines, or internet sites are permitted as sources; only books, scholarly journal articles, or scholarly reference works are allowed.

Honor: **Your Plagiarism Pledge**

Before you turn your paper in, you should write on page four, "I know that plagiarism is the unacknowledged use of someone else's words or ideas, and I pledge that this paper is not plagiarized" and sign it. A plagiarized paper will receive a zero.

THIRD PAPER: A REVOLUTIONARY CHARACTER

Elby-Scrivner 1

Bart Elby-Scrivner

Ms. Taches

English Honors

8 March 2008

William Blake: Child and Lamb

William Blake (1757-1827) is perhaps best known for his poem "The Tiger": "Tiger, tiger, burning bright / In the forests of the night, / What immortal hand or eye / Could frame thy fearful symmetry?" (Blake 263) but his importance in western intellectual history extends far beyond that poem. William Blake is a figure of unique accomplishment, being the only artist to acheive greatness and influence both as a poet and as a painter. Blake is prominently included in anthologies of great poetry and great painting. The question is: what is the common element of influence in his poetry and painting?

We can use a slash to indicate the start of a new line in a poem.

Robert Pipingwild, professor of literature at Mistic University says that all of Blake's influence on modern thought traces back to the profound mysticism that governed Blake's experience of religion:

> Blake was not the typical believer. His whole sense of reality was governed by the tangible perception of spirits, angels, and demons who appeared before his eyes, walked into his rooms, and looked in his windows. For Blake, creativity was a matter of psychological survival. (Pipingwild, 74)

Pipingwild's view is seconded by Forest Hammerchain, the author of <u>In the Blake of an Eye</u>, a biographical examination of Blake's work. According to Hammerchain, Blake "existed in a private reality that was neither insanity nor sanity; he did not see the public world that others saw, but he lived practically in it" (Hammerchain 104). Hammerchaain's ... Blake disarmed public concern about his visionary ... them into paintings and ... entional

Elby-Scrivner 4

Works Cited

Blake, William. <u>Songs of Innocence</u>. New York: Halfcourt, 1992

Hammerchain, Forest. <u>In the Blake of an Eye</u>. Atlanta: Bignet, 2008.

Pipingwild, Robert. "Contemporary Views of William Bl...

Piping down th...

Assignment Three: Think like an academic writer — about words.

We continue training our minds to perceive the power of academic words. Great writers use these words not only with precise meaning but also in precise positions. Often the power word is the last word in the sentence; it is put there, like a punch-line in a joke, and it pops in at the last point, in the spotlight of the period.

Great writers also pay attention to the poetic sounds of the vowels and consonants in words, using words with soft consonants for soft ideas and words with punchy consonants such as *d*'s, *b*'s, and *k*'s to give more impact. In the vocabulary below, notice the *k* sound and the hissy end in the adjective *vacuous*, or the crispness of the verb *disclose*. You should read and study poetry in order to train your ear, particularly traditional poetry in which the control of sound is intense. My poetry textbook *Poetry and Humanity* provides a strong background in these elements.

Formal academic words have a different tone from colloquial words; often, they come from Latin and have a crisp, logical sound—different from many words that come from Greek. The word *penultimate* is from Latin, and the word *phenomenon* is from Greek. Of course, many of our power words come from Greek too.

	Word	Definition	Part of Speech	Example
11.	**prolific**	productive	adjective	Dickinson was a **prolific** poet.
11.	**soporific**	sleep-inducing	adjective	The **soporific** speech put us to sleep.
12.	**idiosyncrasy**	peculiarity	noun	That odd mannerism was an **idiosyncrasy**.
12.	**bon mot**	witticism	noun	Oscar Wilde uttered a classic **bon mot**.
13.	**penultimate**	next to last	adjective	His **penultimate** novel was a failure.
13.	**vacuous**	stupid	adjective	His comments were **vacuous** and boring.
14.	**malevolent**	malicious	adjective	Boo was described as a **malevolent** phantom.
14.	**disclose**	reveal	verb	Plath did not **disclose** the poem's meaning.
15.	**indolent**	lazy	adjective	Like other **indolent** writers, he failed.
15.	**effulgence**	radiance	noun	They lauded him with effulgent praise.

Discussion Questions

Which of these words might be used in a science paper? Which might be found in a poem? Which of these words might be good to describe a revolutionary character?

Assignment Three: Think like an academic writer — about sentences.

The initial strangeness that we sometimes feel with grammar is only a result of grammar being new to us. Like everything else, once you get used to grammar, the strangeness goes away. It becomes perfectly familiar, and then you enjoy it and build things with it, like a set of blocks. At some point you realize just how much clarity grammar gives you; it makes the unknown parts of your thinking visible, and you can set them up the way you like them. Think about this: knowing what you are doing is always more fun than not knowing what you are doing. Reflect on this sentence taken from *4Practice, Volume One*:

	The	**anthropomorphic**	gods	loved	influencing	the	**bellicose**	Greeks'	lives.
Parts of Speech	adj.	adj.	n.	v.	n.	adj.	adj.	adj.	n.
Parts of Sentence			subj.	AVP	----------------------------D.O.----------------------------				
Phrases					----------------------gerund phrase----------------------				
Clauses	-----------------one independent clause-----------------								
	a simple declarative sentence								

Grammar: The direct object is a gerund phrase built on the gerund *influencing*. The noun *lives* is the object of the gerund.

Vocabulary: The adjective *anthropomorphic* means man-shaped, shaped like a human being; *anthropo* means man, and *morph* means shape. The adjective *bellicose* means warlike; *bell* means war.

Poetics: The sentence ends in a strong spondee, *Greeks' lives*; a spondee is two stressed syllables in a row. Notice the alliteration of *gods* and *Greeks*.

Writing: Verbal phrases—in this case a gerund phrase—allow us to put more energy into our sentences by injecting active verbiness into parts of sentences that are ordinarily nouns. This makes writing more dynamic.

Punctuation: The apostrophe comes after the *s* in *Greeks'* because it is making the plural *Greeks* possessive: a Greek's shield, some Greeks' shields.

Students could study this page as homework, to be followed by a short quiz at the beginning of class.

Assignment Three: Focus Areas — Actual Research Paper Comments

We have already seen twenty comments archived from two decades of actual comments on student research papers; here are ten more. When you write your third paper, review the first twenty, and then concentrate intensely on these comments as well. Pretend that it is you who made these errors, and that you will never let it happen again.

1. You have a pronoun reference error: THIS as the subject.
Please avoid using the demonstrative pronoun this as the subject of a sentence. Use it as an adjective, referring to this idea, this policy, this poem. When you just say "this altered everything," there is almost always ambiguity, leaving the reader to wonder what this you mean.

2. You have a compound subject/verb disagreement. s/v
You have a subject/verb disagreement caused by a compound subject. Remember that a compound subject joined by and is plural because it means both: Smith and Jones write. A compound subject joined by *or* is singular because it means only one: Smith or Jones writes. A compound subject joined by or but that contains a plural noun as the second subject is plural: Smith or the Joneses are here. As a fundamental principal of grammar, the verb must always agree with the subject.

3. You have a title spelling error. sp
My mark sp means that you have a spelling error. Certain spelling errors are remarkably common, including misspelling of the main word of the paper and in the title of the paper, or in the first paragraph, because it never occurs to you that you could make a spelling error so obvious or so soon! Always double-check these details.

4. You have a split infinitive.
It is best to word your sentences as to avoid split infinitives. Splitting an infinitive means inserting an adverb between the two words of the infinitive form of a verb. If we take the infinitive to see, and split it with the adverb vividly, we have to vividly see, which is a split infinitive. It is better to put the adverb after the infinitive: to see vividly. Instead of writing that Aristophanes's criticism allowed Athenians "to not only see that he was a better writer," write "not only to see." Instead of "to more wisely select," write "to select more wisely." Put adverbial material outside the infinitive, where it will not split the infinitive.

Ask students to explain which of these errors they are most likely to make.

5. You used an elementary encyclopedia in your Works Cited.
There are several types of sources that you should really not emphasize as sources in your Works Cited. One is the elementary encyclopedia, such as World Book or Americana. These are not respectable as research sources because you do not have to search for anything: the material is pre-searched and listed in a single place alphabetically. Furthermore, the articles in encyclopedias are written at a universal, elementary level, and only skim the surface of the subject in the briefest way. You will not learn much there, but you might get some initial ideas for real research by reading an encyclopedia article. A second source of material that you should avoid is the Cliff's Notes or Monarch's Notes sort of pre-digested analysis. These booklets are literary analysis at its lowest level and are not respected as research sources. You would be far better off to seek out important biographies and noted works of literary criticism. A final source that you must avoid is the slip, or jacket cover, blurb on a book. To quote from a slip is to suggest that you have only skimmed the surface, and did not take the time to delve inside the book. Develop the ability to discover advanced sources of information in the library and bookstore.

6. Avoid self-reference.
Avoid self-reference--focus on the thesis. It is important to avoid self-reference of all forms when writing a formal paper. By self-reference, I mean referring to yourself in the first person singular (I), referring to the paper itself (In this paper I intend . . .), or even referring to quotations you have presented as quotations (This quotation means that . . .). Why should you avoid self-reference? Well, when you point to something, you want a person to look at the thing, and not at your hand. Mentioning yourself, your paper, or your quotations only breaks the reader's concentration by drawing attention away from the ideas and toward the medium. Don't break the spell; get the reader thinking about Sophocles, and keep the reader thinking about Sophocles.

In other words, do not unintentionally write papers about themselves; intentionally write papers about ideas.

This does not mean that you do not include your own thinking in your paper. It only means that you present your ideas without referring to yourself in the first person. Just present the idea; you do not need to say that it is you thinking because your name at the top of the page informs us whose views these are, if they are not documented as being the views of someone else.

The self-reference comment is an important, advanced point.

7. You have an over-reliance on one source.
When most of the quotes in a research paper are from a single source, especially if they are from only a few pages of a single source or if they are presented in page-number order from a single source, this gives the reader the impression that the paper is not a research paper but a book report. For best effect, you need to present the reader with a diverse collection of research evidence, avoiding the impression that you relied too much on one or two sources.

8. Your title is not accurate.
Write an accurate title for your paper. As I have discussed in class, the title of a formal paper should be true, precise, and specific. It should be, probably, a thumbnail expression of the thesis, rather than a mere general categorical term. A paper on imagery in Hamlet, therefore, should not be titled "Shakespeare," but should be "Imagery in Shakespeare's Hamlet." If a title is too broad, it is actually false because the paper does not really discuss what the title promises, but only a small portion of it. Please write an accurate title for your next paper.

9. Enclose appositives in commas.
Punctuate appositives correctly. It is good to use appositives--interrupting definitions--to insert information gracefully into sentences, especially early in a research paper when you might be mentioning names or titles unfamiliar to the reader, but remember that appositives take TWO COMMAS or none--usually two, and you must not forget the second appositive comma: Ted Hughes, Plath's former husband, wrote in praise of Plath's writings. Charles VIII, King of France, invaded and conquered Italy.

10. Punctuate dashes and hyphens correctly.
Please notice exactly the difference between the way dashes and hyphens are made. In professional publishing a true dash is simply a longer mark than a hyphen (It looks like this—not this-see?), but in Courier type font, a dash is a two-hyphen mark used to indicate abrupt breaks in thought--like that, whereas a hyphen is a one-stroke mark used to glue two words into one-thought units. Some manuals suggest that you make a dash with two blank spaces and only one hyphen - like that, but do not. Use two hyphens and no spaces for a dash, and one hyphen and no spaces for a hyphen, and then there is no doubt which mark you really intended. Remember the logic that a dash is a break but a hyphen is glue.

Assignment Three • Revolutionary Character

Purpose: An Intense Nonfiction Exploration

All too often, our reading of nonfiction is confined to history textbooks and other works that offer only general summaries of information. One of the pleasures of the educated life is reading real biographies that take us deeply into the lives of famous people. This assignment will send you to the nonfiction section, most notably the biography section, of the library, where you can continue to explore what the library has to offer in printed books and journals.

Topic: A Revolutionary Character

Your paper will be about a famous individual whom you regard as a revolutionary character, a person who dramatically changed the world. There have been evil individuals who changed the world for the worse, but in this assignment you will focus on a revolutionary hero, someone you admire, someone who broke new ground, someone who brought knowledge, healing, justice, beauty, or equality to the world. Your teacher may put additional limits on the topic if he or she wants to focus deeply on famous individuals who are a part of your curriculum.

Your paper must not be a short biography, beginning with the person's life and ending with the death. You should focus on the reason the person is revolutionary. This does not mean that you must use the word *revolutionary* or the word *hero*.

There is one more twist. The individual you select must have died before 1950 and must be the subject of an article in *Encyclopedia Britannica* or similar serious reference work.

Most of the specifications for this paper remain unchanged; the main difference is in the topic and in the sources required. Your teacher will provide you with additional guidelines that connect the assignment to your other coursework.

Emphasize that this paper may not be organized chronologically, like an encyclopedia article; it must be an essay.

Length: Three pages

This paper must be no more than three pages long, with a fourth page for the Works Cited. Page three should not be almost blank; it should contain a half-page or more of text.

Due Date: Your teacher will assign the due date, providing at least two weeks for both research and writing. Late papers will lose one letter grade per day.

Format: MLA

This will be an MLA essay with long and short quotations. A paper done in any other format will be returned to the student to be redone. The teacher may assign a letter-grade-per-day penalty for lateness in such a case. The paper should be typed on one side of the page only, in ragged-right, double-spaced Courier type font, ten or twelve point size. There must be a minimum of one long quotation and three short quotations in the paper.

Structure: Essay

This paper should be a three-part thesis essay, with introduction, body, and conclusion. The paragraphs should be organized and clearly connected. Use a key word from your thesis to connect the paper.

Source: Five Sources Required

For this third paper at least five sources must be listed in your Works Cited page. Each must be quoted or cited somewhere in your paper. No elementary encyclopedias, popular magazines, or internet sites are permitted as sources; only books, scholarly journal articles, or scholarly reference works are allowed.

Honor: Your Plagiarism Pledge

Before you turn your paper in, you should write on page four, "I know that plagiarism is the unacknowledged use of someone else's words or ideas, and I pledge that this paper is not plagiarized" and sign it. A plagiarized paper will receive a zero.

FOURTH PAPER: AN ABSTRACT CONCEPT

Phimm 1

Sarah Phimm

Mr. Ree

English Honors

14 May 2006

Whitman's Song Changed Poetry

It is not often that one individual has such an impact on on a creative field that the field is never the same again, that everyone involved in the field, and indeed the world at large, views the field with different eyes. There have been a number of great poets in American history, but only one has changed the very nature of poetry, not just in the United States but in the world, making it impossible to go back, and that is Walt Whitman.

According to Henry David, Thorow Professor of Literature at Blake University, when Walt Whitman wrote Leaves of Grass, he:

> . . . was no mere pioneer of modern poetry, he invented modern poetry, like Euclid founded mathematics or Herodotus invented history. Whitehead once said that the entire history of western thought is based on Plato, and I would add that Whitman is the Plato of modern poetry. Before Whitman the traditions of poetry had ossified, but he delineated a new poetic world. (David 74)

The ellipsis shows that we are not quoting from the beginning of the sentence. We do not need to do this in a short quote.

This view of Whitman as the father of modern verse is the standard view. Eleanor Radcliffe agrees: "Walt Whitman laid the foundation for the poetry we write today. He broke the mold. Whitman was not only before his time, he was from a different artistic cosmos than the poets of his time and before" (Radcliffe 73). F.G. Leghorn says that "Whitman changed everything. If you want to see the shift in poetry, look at any anthology ...efore-poetry and the after-poetry" (Leghorn 134).

...hat Whitman transformed the art of

...do to poetry,

Works Cited

Phimm 4

David, Henry. Whitman Sang My Song. New York: Halfcourt, 1992.

Leghorn, F.G. "How Walt Whitman Changed the Landscape of Poetry." Introduction. Modern Poetry and the Song of Ourselves, Chicago: Addem UP, 2003.

Radcliffe, Eleanor. The Conceptual Foundations of Modern Poetry. Atlanta: Bignet, 2008.

---. Primary Themes in Poetry since 18...

Assignment Four: Think like an academic writer — about words.

One of the biggest problems students have when they begin to write academic papers is that they try to use vocabulary that is beyond their vocabulary development level. They sometimes think that academic writing must be filled with big, impressive words, and they load their sentences with words that sound intellectual, not realizing that they are misusing the words and making the paper sound amateurish. This problem can be worse if a student avoids looking words up in a dictionary. Yes, we want you to increase your command of great vocabulary, but you have to do the work: look the words up, study their grammar and usage.

Furthermore, good academic writers do not overuse strong vocabulary. They do not attempt to sound impressive by forcing big words into sentences. The goal is not to sound impressive; it is to be clear. Use big words sparingly; if there are too many in a sentence, they compete with each other.

Think about this: if you succeed in sounding impressive, you draw the reader's attention toward you, which is not where you want it. If you are writing a paper about Alexander, you want the reader's mind on Alexander, not on you. Being impressive is not a goal; teach us something about Alexander, and we will be impressed.

	Word	Definition	Part of Speech	Example
16.	**anthology**	collection	noun	We read an **anthology** of poetry.
16.	**incoherent**	confusing	adjective	The paper was completely **incoherent**.
17.	**commensurate**	in proportion	adjective	The reward was **commensurate** with the task.
17.	**acrimony**	bitterness	noun	He felt no **acrimony** towards Coleridge.
18.	**ossify**	turn to bone	verb	His thinking had **ossified** into inflexibility.
18.	**xenophobic**	afraid of foreigners	adjective	The book was a **xenophobic** diatribe.
19.	**pathos**	pity	noun	The story evoked understanding and **pathos**.
19.	**gravamen**	essence	noun	I understood the **gravamen** of her story.
20.	**delineate**	to outline	verb	He quickly **delineated** the plan.
20.	**melancholy**	deep sadness	noun	Her death plunged Werther into **melancholy**.

Discussion Questions

If you could only remember two of these words, which two would you choose? Why? Which word in this list sounds most intelligent?

Assignment Four: Think like an academic writer — about sentences.

If you want to be an excellent academic writer, you must be excellent at grammar. This means that you must like grammar because it is almost impossible to be good at something you do not like. When you do not like something, you do not put your mind on it the same way. Fortunately, when you really know grammar, you see how wonderful it is. Reflect on this sentence taken from *4Practice, Volume One*:

	Socrates	refuses	**expatriation**;	instead,	he	chooses	execution.
Parts of Speech	n.	v.	n.	adv.	pron.	v.	n.
Parts of Sentence	subj.	AVP	D.O.		subj.	AVP	D.O.
Phrases	no prepositional, appositive, or verbal phrases						
Clauses	----------------independent clause-----------------				-----------------independent clause--------------------		
	an I;I compound declarative sentence						

Grammar: The sentence features two independent clauses, perfectly balanced. Each clause has an action verb that passes the action to a direct object. This sentence illustrates the strong compound logic that demands a compound sentence.

Vocabulary: An expatriate is a banished person; to expatriate is to banish; the idea is that one is out of the fatherland; *ex* means out, and *patr* means father. We also use the word for individuals who voluntarily leave their homeland to live abroad, rather than having been exiled.

Poetics: Notice the internal rhymes of *refuses* and *chooses*, and of *expatriation* and *execution*. The *oosh* sound in *execution* works with *refuses* and *chooses*.

Writing: The striking quality of this sentence is its perfect parallelism of both grammar and sound.

Punctuation: This is the classic place for a semicolon: between two independent clauses in a compound sentence that does not have a coordinating conjunction to join the clauses.

Assignment Four: Focus Areas — Actual Research Paper Comments

We have already seen twenty comments archived from actual comments on student research papers; here are ten more. When you write your third paper, review the first twenty, and then concentrate intensely on these comments as well. Pretend that it is you who made these errors, and that you will never let it happen again.

1. You use the wrong word (w)
Choose your words carefully. My mark w means that you have used the wrong word. It is easy to use a word that sounds impressive but that has a wrong or even absurd meaning in your sentence. If, for example, you say that "Sinclair's family sided with the movements of the Confederacy," I wonder what you mean. Political movements? Military movements? In this case movements would seem to be the wrong word for your sentence. You could leave it out: "Sinclair's family sided with the Confederacy." Or you could change it to something more direct: "Sinclair's family sided with the states/arguments/opinions of the Confederacy." Be wary of picking words for their sound; sense comes first.

2. You have an indentation error. (5> 10>)
Indent paragraphs, long quotes, and Works Cited properly. A 5> or a 10> mark means that you should have indented the line five spaces or the quote ten spaces. In accordance with the MLA instructions, we put exactly five blank spaces at the beginning of a paragraph, and we start typing on the sixth space. We put exactly ten blank spaces before each line of a long quotation, and we start typing on the eleventh space. The second line, not the first, of each Works Cited listing should be indented five spaces. You can indent by hitting the space bar repeatedly, but it is easier to set your tabs at the fifth and tenth space.

3. Use ragged-right margin, not justified.
Use a ragged-right margin. Please do not justify the right margin of your paper. Instead, use a ragged-right margin, set approximately one inch from the right edge. Even though a justified margin is beautiful, it distorts the spacing of words within the lines, and I cannot then tell whether or not you have made spacing errors.

4. Punctuate dates correctly. (1800s)
In punctuating the names of centuries, such as the 1800s or the 1900s, do not insert an apostrophe before the *s*. For example, you should type 1700s rather than 1700's. This is correct: "During the 1970s Borges returned to writing fiction."

5. Follow the MLA rules for the title of your paper.

Construct your title correctly. Please review the MLA requirements for the title of the paper. The title should be exactly centered, should be double-spaced, should not be in ALL CAPS, should have the First Letter of Each Major Word--but not prepositions or articles--Capitalized, and should not be underlined, unless you underline to indicate a book title or something else that belongs in italics. You should only double-space down to the title from the date above, and you should double-space down to the first paragraph from the title. If you use both a title and subtitle, use a colon and a blank space between them: H.G. Wells: Master of Science Fiction. If the title takes up more than one line, break the title at an appropriate mid-point, rather than have just one word or two on the second line, and double-space between the two lines of the title.

6. Punctuate the apostrophe in possessives correctly.

Learn to use possessive apostrophes correctly. We always make a noun, singular or plural, possessive by ADDING something to it. We make singular nouns possessive by adding an apostrophe and an s, even when the noun already ends in s. Thus, we would type poetess's, not poetess'; Euripides's, not Euripides'; Dickens's, not Dickens' or worse Dicken's; Herodotus's, not Herodotus'; and Sophocles's, not Sophocles'. If the noun is plural instead of singular, then we simply add the apostrophe: the dogs' houses, many authors' ideas.

In no case would we take a plural noun such as authors or a proper noun such as Socrates and insert an apostrophe into it because the noun ends in s: Socrate's! Apostrophes never mutilate words. We form possessives only by ADDING either an apostrophe or an apostrophe and an s. The possessive of the proper noun Parmenides is Parmenides's, not Parmenide's; the sophist's name was not Parmenide!

Caution: Do not use apostrophes in ordinary plurals that are not possessive: "Epictetus taught that ordinary philosopher's were free" is an error because no apostrophe should be used; the word philosophers should be an ordinary plural common noun.

By the way, some style manuals would allow you to drop the s after singular possessives, but I would prefer that you do not; I prefer the old-fashioned way, which is also preferred by MLA and by Strunk and White in their classic writing text, The Elements of Style.

Phimm, 4

Works Cited

Rushing, Bertram. Socrates's Influence on Modern Philosophers. New York: Halfcourt, 1998.

Tottle, Aris. Herodotus's Effect on History. Los Angeles: U of Absalom P, 1995.

---. Introduction.

7. Use correct commas in year, city, nation.
Please remember that the year, city, and nation are often used as appositives and therefore require commas before and after. Thus, we say "August 20, 1947, was hot" or "Dublin, Ireland, is damp" or "Chicago, Illinois, is busy" and we are required to put the second comma in each case. Failure to put the second comma usually warps the meaning of the sentence, because it makes the second word, rather than the first, the subject of a verb. What if someone asks where I am going, and I answer, "Chicago, Illinois is my home." That means I'm going to Chicago, but my home is somewhere in Illinois. If I answer, "Chicago, Illinois, is my home," then that means Chicago is my home. To change commas is to change meanings. Put a comma before and after an appositive.

8. Underline things as such.
Underline when you are referring to a word itself. Please remember that words, numbers, and letters as such must be placed in italics, which means--on a typewriter--that they must be underlined (NOT put in quotation marks!). In this way we distinguish the word dog from the animal, dog. We use b's in spelling, and we use 3's in counting. See? We also place foreign language words in italics/underline: Homer begins his story in medias res, in the middle of things. This technique will be especially important when you are analyzing poetry or literature and are making reference to the words, letters, or sounds contained in the writing. Be especially sure to avoid the common mistake of putting words as such in quotation marks; we do not refer to the word "shibboleth" but to the word shibboleth.

9. Put no comma in parentheticals.
Do not put commas in the parenthetical documentary notes. In an MLA-style parenthetical documentary notation, we do not put a comma between the author's name and the page number. The note should look like this (Euripides 64) rather than like this (Euripides, 64).

10. Space your parenthetical notes correctly. (#)
Space correctly before parenthetical notes for long and short quotations. My # mark means that you have made a spacing error in a parenthetical documentary note. Remember that spaces are language objects, just as letters are. You have to get them right. When you use a short quotation, first give the quotation in quotation marks, and skip ONE space before the documentary note "like this" (Thompson 78). "Do not omit the space like this"(Thompson 78) or put two spaces "like this" (Thompson 78).

> On long quotations, skip TWO spaces after the period at the end of the quotation before you type the documentary note. It should look like this. (Thompson 78)

Assignment Four • A Concept or Theory

Purpose: Deep Exploration of an Abstract Concept

In each academic field there are concepts that attempt to explain and integrate diverse phenomena into a single concept. In science, for example, there is gravitation, a force so mysterious that its actions seem almost impossible. In history there are theories that attempt to explain events in terms of economics. The purpose of this paper is to send you to the library once again, and to cause you to do some deep reading and thinking, not this time about a concrete subject such as a person or a book, but about an abstract concept.

Topic: An Academic Concept

Your paper will present an academic concept. The concept can come from any field: science, history, art, poetry, literature, or any other. You will likely discuss the origin and importance of the concept, and present evidence for or against it. You might discuss the current state of acceptance of the concept; has it now been refuted or rejected? There are fascinating ideas that were dominant in the past but that are now known to be false, and these would be interesting topics.

One limit: do not select any type of (phony) pseudo-science, such as the so-called Bermuda Triangle (there is no such thing; the BT is just a science fiction myth that promoters use to make money by fooling people). If you are going to choose a scientific concept, use real science.

Depending upon your curriculum, your teacher may limit you to ideas within a particular academic field and give you suggestions for concept topics.

Length: Three pages

This paper must be no more than three pages long, with a fourth page for the Works Cited. Page three should contain a half-page or more of text.

Due Date: Your teacher will assign the due date, providing at least two weeks for both research and writing. Late papers will lose one letter grade per day.

Format: MLA

This will be an MLA essay with long and short quotations. A paper done in any other format will be returned to the student to be redone. The teacher may assign a letter-grade-per-day penalty for lateness in such a case. The paper should be typed on one side of the page only, in ragged-right, double-spaced Courier type font, ten or twelve point size. There must be a minimum of one long quotation and three short quotations in the paper.

Structure: Essay

This paper should be a three-part thesis essay, with introduction, body, and conclusion. The paragraphs should be organized and clearly connected. Use a key word from your thesis to connect the paper.

Source: Five Sources Required

For this fourth paper at least five sources must be listed in your Works Cited page. Each must be quoted or cited somewhere in your paper. No elementary encyclopedias, popular magazines, or internet sites are permitted as sources; only books, scholarly journal articles, or scholarly reference works are allowed.

Honor: Your Plagiarism Pledge

Before you turn your paper in, you should write on page four, "I know that plagiarism is the unacknowledged use of someone else's words or ideas, and I pledge that this paper is not plagiarized" and sign it. A plagiarized paper will receive a zero.

Phimm 1

Sarah Phimm

Mr. Ree

English Honors

14 May 2006

Do not capitalize title.

S/V

WHITMAN'S SONG CHANGED POETRY

Each of the notable modern poets have contributed in some significant way to the progress of poetry as an art form. It is not often that one individual has such an impact on on a creative field that the field is never the same again, that everyone involved in the field, and indeed the world at large, view the field with different eyes. There have been many great poets in American history but only one has changed the very nature

S/V

Advanced Writing Hide-and-Seek

Here is a three-page sample paper (and Works Cited page), that has errors hidden in it. The errors may have been explained anywhere in this book. Your task is to find every error. I will not tell you how many there are because when you have to proofread your own paper, you do not begin knowing how many errors there are. The purpose is to intensify your proofreading vision and to establish a deep impression of just how perfect advanced English is expected to be.

Your teacher may assign this project before you write your final paper, or afterwards, or as a project that you work on slowly from the beginning of the text. It might be assigned as an individual project or as a group project; that is up to your teacher. I have added line numbers to the display so that you can easily refer to the errors by line number. Your teacher may decide to copy the next three pages for you, so that you can mark errors on the copy.

In some ways this is a good paper. It has an interesting topic and a good essay structure, but it is filled with inexcusable errors of English and even of MLA format. I would not be able to give this paper a passing grade; the basic English is not negotiable. I do not, however, see why this student might not make an *A* on his next paper, if he proofreads his paper next time.

One more thing: the information in this paper is true; phlogiston was a leading concept advocated by Joseph Priestley and disproven by Lavoisier. The scholars listed in the Works Cited, however, are once again fictional, as are their books and their publishing companies.

Instructions:

1. Do not write in this book; it is not a disposable workbook.
2. On your own paper, list the errors. Give the line number first, and then an explanation.

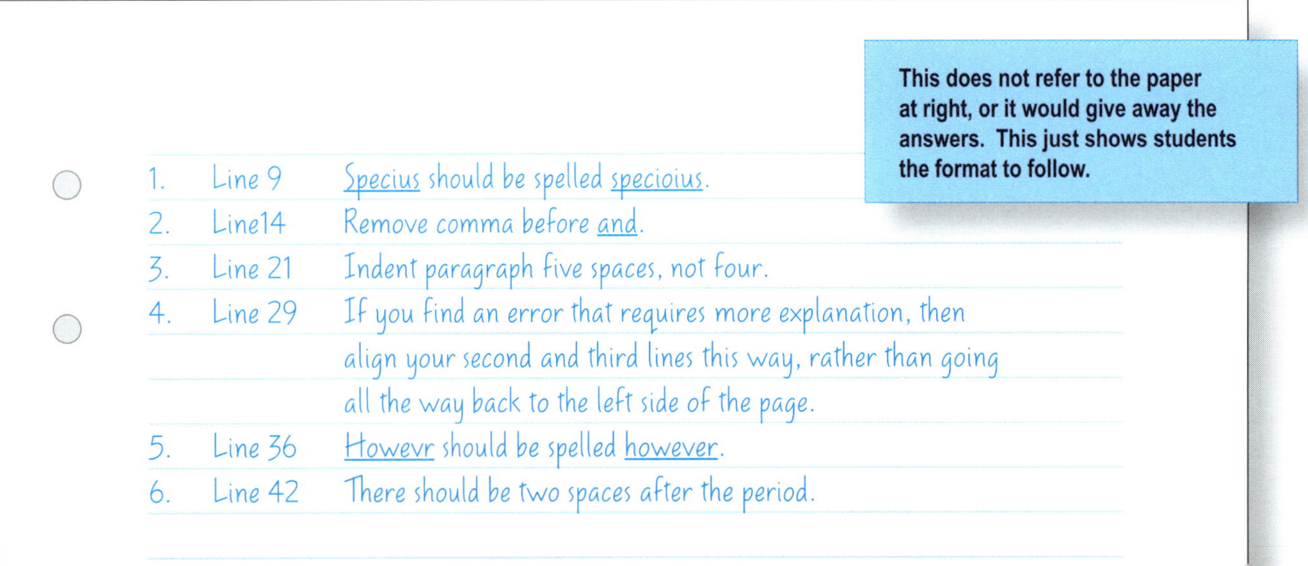

Lowing 1

Bill Lowing

Ms. Sellanius

English Honors

9 January 2005

The Scientific Rejection of Phlogiston

Intellectual history records a number of concepts that were confidently accepted in their day, only to prove specious, when evidence accumulated. In the seventeenth and eighteenth centuries, scientists believed in phlogiston, supposedly an element that was released from solid matter during combustion. The concept of phlogiston traces back to the work of Johann Becher in the late 1600's, but the name *phlogiston* was coined in 1718 by a studnet of Becher's, Georg Ernst Stahl, based on the ancient Greek word *phlogios*, fiery. Professor Arnold Schwartzinator, in his text *Phlogiston Will Be Back*, argues that the "rise and fall of the myth of phlogiston illustrates the ability of the scientific method to expose false concepts eventually," (Schwartzinator, 82).

The rise of phlogiston as a persuasive concept is understandable. Scientist's of the seventeenth century guessed that combustion was an important chemical concept and they could see that the ash remaining after a fire, had far less mass than the object had before the combustion. What, they wondered, happened to the rest of the matter? Not knowing that oxidation--including fire, rusting, and even breathing--was a reaction of an object with the oxygen in the air, they developed a name for the mysterious missing material. Invisible and odorless, scientists called it *phlogiston*. There are many names, however, for mythical and fictional phenomena, and even though it was a false phenomena, phlogiston was difficult to disprove. Ann Drew-Jackson at the Manute Institute of Technology says:

> Advocates of phlogiston had the advantage; they were difficult to silence because phlogiston was, by there fortunate definition, undetectable. It was said to be odorless, colorless, tasteless, weightless, and so when no one could find it, advocates claimed the theory had been confirmed! (Drew-Jackson 11)

Lowing 2

These advocates, included Joseph Priestley (1733-1804), one of the greatest scientists of the eighteenth century. Priestley discovered oxygen, invented soda water and staunchly supported the concept of phlogiston. In 1796, Priestley wrote:

> There have been few, if any, revolutions in science so great, so sudden, and so general, as the prevalence of what is now usually termed *the new system of chemistry*, or that of the Antiphlogistians, over the doctrine of Stahl, which was at one time thought to have been the greatest discovery that had ever been made in the science. I remember hearing Mr. Peter Woulfe, whose knowlege of chemistry will not be questioned, say that there had hardly been any thing that deserved to be called a *discovery* subsequent to it (Priestley 54).

Priestley dealt with phlogiston's undetectability as best he could. He admitted that the phlogiston theory had it's difficulties: "we are not able to ascertain the weight of phlogiston . . . but neither do any of us pretend to have weighed lite, or the element of heat, though we do not doubt that they are properly substances" (55). Priestley's stubborn adherence to phlogiston, and refusal to embrace the "new system of chemistry" would eventually damage his reputation.

If the rise of phlogiston had been seen as the "greatest discovery that had ever been made" in chemistry the fall of phlogiston was also spectacular. The exposure of phlogiston as a myth would come from Antoine Laurent Lavoisier (1743-1794). A French nobelman with a genius for chemistry (and other fields as well).Priestley may have discovered oxygen, but Lavoisier named both oxygen and hydrogen, and he is now recognized as the father of modern chemistry; it was him who first stated the law of conservation of mass. In a 1783 paper Lavoisier describes an experiment in which he used seeled containers to show that the mass resulting from chemical reactions such as combustion are equal to the mass before the reaction; in other words, most of the mass missing after combustion

Lowing, 3

does not, as the phlogiston theory supposed, transform itself into some weightless phantom substance but instead is converted into gasses with the mass and weight you would expect. It was a spectacular scientific experiment that any other laboratory could reproduce, and verify, and with it the theory of phlogiston fell from the theoretical heaven. The story of Lavoisier does not end well; his contribution's to intellectual history did not impress the leaders of the French Revolution. In 1794 they tried Lavoisier for treason, and sent him to the guillotine. Lavoisiers' biographer, Will DeBeest, describes how the:

> . . . philistine judge in Lavoisier's trial was indifferent to his contributions to science. When Lavoisier's friends asked the judge to spare his life, he replied, obtusely, "The Republic needs neither scientists nor chemists. The course of justice cannot be delayed."(Debeest 278)

Here we see a quotation within a quotation.

Intellectual history provided for Lavoisier the justice that the sanguinary judge of the French Revolution would not: the concept of phlogiston would fall rapidly from grace, giving weigh to new, more precise and quantitative methods of scientific verification. The concept of phlogiston seemed, in light of the knowledge of it's time, to really explain a mystery. It had the support of the leading scientists, including Joseph Priestley. Even powerful theories however, as Lavoisier demonstrated, cannot stand against those small, but invincible phenomena: facts. By proving that the products of combustion has weight, and that this is a fact, and that therefore phlogiston is a specious concept, Lavoisier led the way for modern chemistry.

Lowing 4

WORKS CITED

LC - do not cap

DeBeest, Will. The Light of Lavoisier and the Forces of Darkness in the Eighteenth Century. Chicago: U of Melville P, 2001.

Drew-Jackson, Ann. Introduction. The Historical Foundation of Modern Chemistry. San Francisco: Baybridge UP, 2007.

Priestley, Joseph. A Defense of the Concept of Phlogiston. New York: Bignet Publishing Company, 1981.

Schwartzinator, Arnold. Phlogiston Will Be Back. Indianapolis: Harpoon, 1988.

I know that plagiarism is the unacknowledged use of someone else's words or ideas, and I pledge that this paper is not plagiari...

Bill Lowing

Phimm 1

Sarah Phimm

Mr. Ree

English Honors

14 May 2006

I like your title.

Whitman's Song Changed Poetry

It is not often that one individual has such an impact on on a creative field that the field is never the same again, that everyone involved in the field, and indeed the world at large, views the field with different eyes. There have been a number of great poets in American history, but only one, has changed the very nature of poetry, not just in the United States but in the world, making it impossible to go back, and that is Walt Whitman.

A clear introduction.

According to Henry David, Thorow Professor of Literature at Blake University, when Walt Whitman wrote Leaves of Grass, he:

> . . . was no mere pioneer of modern poetry, he invented modern poetry, like Euclid founded mathematics or Herodotus invented history. Whitehead once said that the entire history of western ... on Plato, and I would add that Whitman is the

This is a relevant quote.

Staple comments to the front of the student's paper.

96

Sarah,

I enjoyed your thoughtful paper on the influence that Walt Whitman has had on modern poetry. Your paper was written in good English, you got your MLA format right, the essay structure--though not perfect--was quite good, and the idea was worthwhile. I think that you understand why Whitman has been such a powerful figure in the history of poetry. Although there are a few improvements I want you to make on the next paper, this was a very fine effort, and I am proud of what you accomplished.

Let's look at a few details that you can improve next time:

Page 2: you put the word languor in quotation marks, but you should underline things as such, not put them in quotation marks. Underline when you are referring to a word itself. Please remember that words, numbers, and letters as such must be placed in italics, which means --on a typewriter--that they must be underlined (NOT put in quotation marks!). In this way we distinguish the word dog from the animal, dog. We use b's in spelling, and we use 3's in counting. See? We also place foreign language words in italics/underline: Homer begins his story in medias res ...

Teacher Supplementary Section

These blue boxes only appear in the Teacher Manual.

Phimm 4

Works Cited

David, Henry. Whitman Sang My Song. New York: Halfcourt, 1992.

Leghorn, F.G. "How Walt Whitman Changed the Landscape of Poetry." Introduction. Modern Poetry and the Song of Ourselves, Chicago: Addem UP, 2003.

Radcliffe, Eleanor. The Conceptual Foundations of Modern Poetry. Atlanta: Bignet, 2008.

---. Primary Themes in Poetry since 1800. St. Paul: Simone, 1998.

Whitman, Walt. The Complete Poetry of Walt Whitman. Los Angeles: Randlehouse, 1995.

I know that plagiarism is the unacknowledged use of someone else's words or ideas, and I pledge that this paper is not plagiarized.

Sarah Phimm

The Intent of This Illustrated Book

Advanced Academic Writing is an elaborately illustrated program for introducing students to the **four basic elements of academic writing** (English, format, essay structure, and idea). Too often, there are not enough example pages in writing texts, but this book *shows* students what advanced papers actually look like. This is a rigorous classical writing program that will prepare motivated students to excel in advanced high school and college courses. If we are not merely to play, but to win this game, then our writing instruction must be of sufficient substance and of sufficiently high standards to have a profound and permanent impact on how students write academic papers.

The overriding concept that students must understand, as they begin to learn academic writing, is the **seriousness** of academic standards. In academic writing the English, the format, and the essay structure are expected to be right. Not close—right. By insisting on real standards from the outset, we do students who have academic dreams the greatest possible favor.

Assumptions

After decades of grading student papers, and seeing how difficult it was to teach students to write and how difficult it was to arrive at a simple, logical, valid, and appropriate way to grade student papers, I came to a set of practical decisions about my goals and assumptions:

1. **A focus on standard academic writing.** We cannot take chances with students' ability to write academically. There are many important genres of writing, but first things must have priority. Before we spend most available class time on less vital writing goals, we must be certain that students can write academic papers, that they can write the papers expected in their academic high school and college classes. In all of these courses, students will have to submit papers in standard academic English, in organized essay structure, with correct grammar, spelling, and punctuation. The academic genre must have our first attention.

2. **An emphasis on short papers**. Grading formal papers for decades showed me that students make the same mistakes in three-page papers that they make in five- or ten-page papers. By limiting the length to three pages in Volume One of this series, we can place the emphasis entirely on quality. Students will have to do some reading and research for each paper, but the assignment will not overwhelm the entire quarter. With fewer pages to fill, we can have a balance of reading time and writing time, and students can concentrate on perfect details of English, MLA format, essay structure, and thesis quality. Furthermore, a three-page paper

puts us as teachers in a better position; we can grade the papers more easily and give our own attention to the same perfection of detail.

3. **An emphasis on multiple papers.** After years of frustration over the slow progress my students were making, I saw that if I were serious about teaching academic writing, I would have to assign more than one major paper. I was giving a large number of short writing experiences in essay tests and response pieces, but I was doing only one major typed academic paper and hoping that the students would be trained by that. One was not working. Writing a formal academic paper is a high-level process, and it cannot be learned in one pass. There is too much to learn. Academic writing involves the application and integration of numerous language elements: grammar, punctuation, essay structure, paragraph structure and connectedness, attention to a standard such as MLA, and the intellectual ability to identify a meaningful academic idea.

I already knew how much work multiple papers would require, both for the students and for me, but I decided that we would just have to do it. I began assigning one major paper per grading term, and as the papers accumulated, I finally began to receive the writing I had hoped for. Each batch of papers was better. Students who got *F*'s or *D*'s on the first paper recollected their attention, and their subsequent papers were dramatically better. Students needed a guided opportunity to get their bad papers out of the way. With each successive paper, they focused on new details. By the end of the year, they had the process under control, and this training had an effect on all of the writing they did in my class and others.

4. **Professional grading.** Whether we like it or not, grading is a fact in most school systems, and it affects the effort students put into an assignment. The only intelligent response to this *fait accompli* is to take advantage of it by assigning academic papers as major grades and by making the grading process thorough, honest, tough, literary, and professional. The grading process must be commensurate with the quality of the writing process; it must be utterly professional but also supportive. We will discuss the grading process in more detail presently.

5. **A tough refusal of sub-grade-level errors.** It is easy for us as teachers to fall into a trap in which we chronically endure the same English mistakes, year after year, with the helpless feeling that it is impossible to teach correct elementary school English. Before we know it, students are still making third grade and fourth grade mistakes in middle school and high school. We must not stand for it, and the students must know that we will not. For the students' future success in academics, it is necessary to break this cycle, but the cycle will never be broken so long as we pamper students, minimizing their very real English errors and bestowing passing

grades for sincere expression. If we want students to progress, to stop making elementary mistakes, we must demand it. We must refuse to pass a paper filled with grammar, spelling, and punctuation mistakes.

In my own classroom, I discovered that once I informed students they would get *F*'s for bad English, and followed through by giving *F*'s, a miracle occurred: the very students who had been unable to write correct English became able. It had been a charade. They had been turning in error-ridden papers because I had been accepting them.

I know that no one grading method is acceptable everywhere. In this text I have explained to the students that you, the teacher, are the boss when it comes to grading. Some schools do not assign letter grades. Some teachers will be in a situation that demands a gentler slope than the one that benefitted my students. In *Advanced Academic Writing*, you can have the best of both worlds; I have presented the rigorous grading policies that I used in advanced middle and high school classes, and that I had to face as a student in college and graduate school; you now have the option of using my presentation to show students what may be ahead of them, while offering them something softer if you see that it is necessary in your situation. Or, you can use my approach as a guideline. You will know what to do.

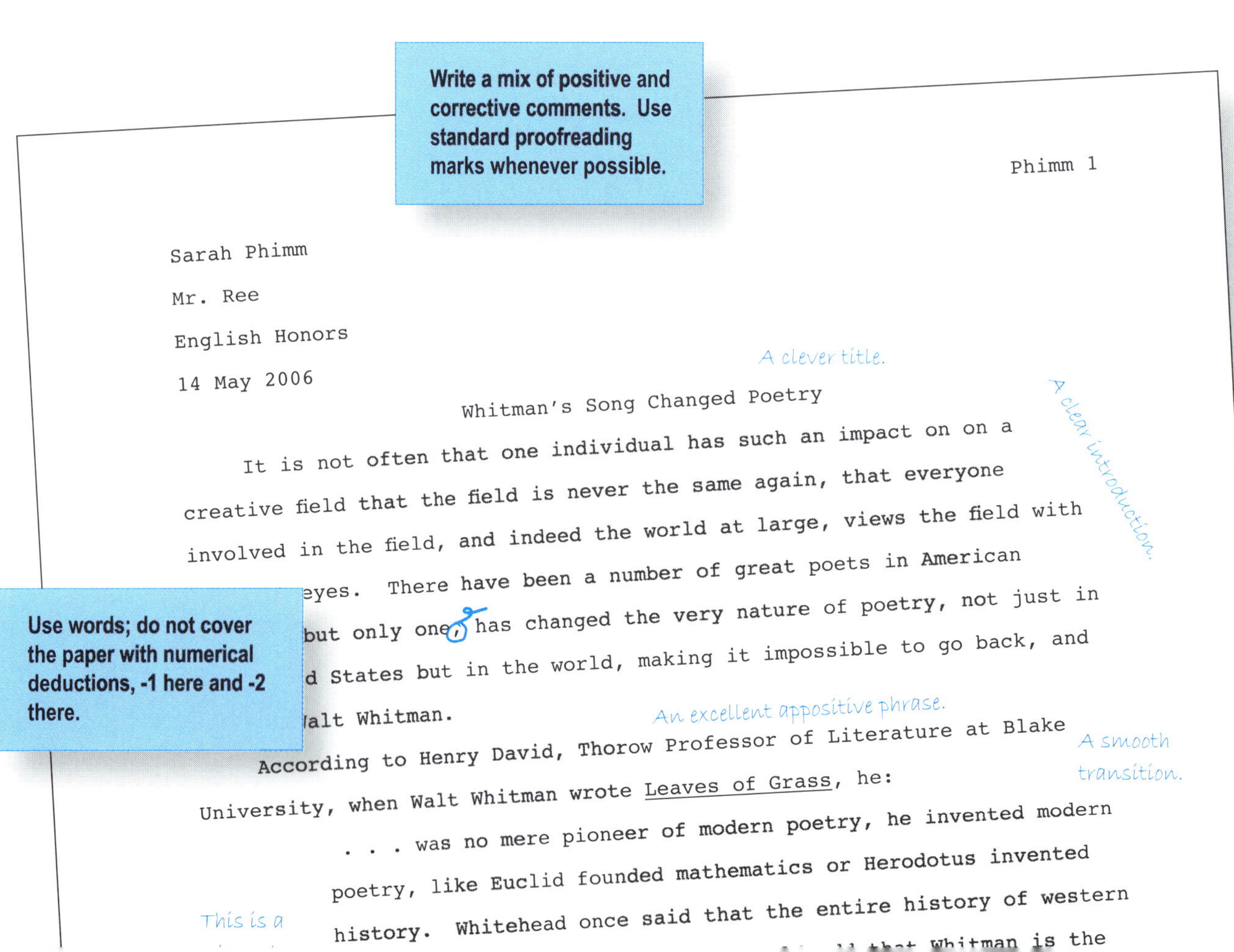
Write a mix of positive and corrective comments. Use standard proofreading marks whenever possible.

Phimm 1

Sarah Phimm

Mr. Ree

English Honors

14 May 2006

A clever title.

Whitman's Song Changed Poetry

A clear introduction.

It is not often that one individual has such an impact on on a creative field that the field is never the same again, that everyone involved in the field, and indeed the world at large, views the field with ...eyes. There have been a number of great poets in American ... but only one, has changed the very nature of poetry, not just in ...d States but in the world, making it impossible to go back, and ...alt Whitman.

Use words; do not cover the paper with numerical deductions, -1 here and -2 there.

An excellent appositive phrase.

According to Henry David, Thorow Professor of Literature at Blake University, when Walt Whitman wrote Leaves of Grass, he:

A smooth transition.

. . . was no mere pioneer of modern poetry, he invented modern poetry, like Euclid founded mathematics or Herodotus invented history. Whitehead once said that the entire history of western

This is a

Implementation: Two Academic Papers per Semester

Like my grammar, vocabulary, and poetics programs, which prepare foundations for this book, this program is not a unit. It too is designed to be a continuous presence in the curriculum. It provides introductory instruction that includes punctuation and usage reference pages, followed by four major writing assignments. For any school that uses quarterly grading terms, it will be easy to schedule one paper per quarter. A school that uses six-week terms can schedule papers in four of the six-week periods or assign additional papers to complete the year. Assuming a quarter system, the implementation might look like this:

Q1	Q2	Q3	Q4
Grammar review. Introduction. First assignment.	Second assignment.	Third assignment.	Fourth assignment.

With this schedule, one of the major grades in each grading term is a formal academic paper. Students cannot give grudging half-attention to the one formal paper of the year. More papers, each one more demanding, are coming, and students will have to master the challenges of each one in order to prepare for the next. Academic writing will become a fact of life.

If you need to do a grammar review with students, it is best to do that before embarking on this program. *The Magic Lens* provides that type of front-loaded, compacted instruction that launches all four levels of grammar at the beginning of the year. Students will need to arrive at this writing book versed in parts of speech, parts of sentence, phrases, and clauses. Students cannot, for example, understand punctuation rules (e.g., put a comma after an introductory dependent clause) if they do not know the four levels of basic grammar. Advanced academic writing is, to a surprising extent, grammar applied.

The introduction to *Advanced Academic Writing* is fifty-eight pages long, but much of it simply provides convenient reference content for use when students want to look up punctuation or usage rules. The main purpose of the introduction is to explain to students the approach, the MLA basics, and the grading philosophy. Much of the introduction can be assigned as homework reading, then discussed in class, with the teacher emphasizing important points. This should take six one-hour lessons, although some of the lessons are shorter and might be combined. The class should go immediately into the first paper after the introduction so that students can work with the ideas of the introduction fresh in their minds.

Here are some suggestions for teaching the introductory content. Modify as required.

Lesson One - Basic Expectations - Pages 4-11

1. Read pages 5-6 aloud together, pausing for comments and questions. Feel free to insert your own comments and explanations or to ask questions as you go. Ask students if they can figure out what each correction on the sample paper on page 4 means, without being told.

2. Have students read pages 7-9 on their own, then go over it together, point by point, making sure students understand why each element is important.

3. Read each paragraph of page 10 aloud, then spend time examining the diagram on page 11; discuss each paragraph on page 10 and locate its details on the diagram on page 11. Do this one paragraph at a time. Check for understanding.

4. Homework: ask students to write a paragraph explaining how an essay structure is different from other forms of writing. In class, have students read their answers aloud, and discuss what the group has observed as a whole.

Lesson Two - MLA Method - Pages 12-19

This lesson is composed of four two-page sets. In each there is text on the left page and a sample page on the right page. Read the text aloud, a paragraph at a time, and pause to examine the details on the illustration at right. Examine each two pages carefully before turning the page.

Lesson Three - A Sample Paper - Pages 20-25

1. Read page 20 aloud together. Then have the students read the sample paper in full silently. When they finish, go through the sample paper one page at a time, and ask students to point out details of the paper that illustrate things they learned in lessons one and two. Finally, ask the students to assess the paper: how good do the students think the paper is?

2. Ask students to read and study pages 23-24. Discuss what students have realized by reading these two pages.

Lesson Four - Punctuation - Pages 26-31

1. Pages 26-29. As a group, examine the rules for each punctuation mark separately. Look first at the comma rules. Ask students to read through the rules, then ask if there are any that they do not understand or that they did not know before. Then do the same with the other marks.

2. Pages 30-31. First, read page 30 aloud together. Then ask students to find all of the punctuation errors on page 31. This should not be graded, unless you give a simple participation grade. It should be open-book so that they can refer back to pages 26-29. They may work in groups of two if you prefer. The teacher manual has errors circled in blue, but the student manual does not. When students think they have found every error, go through the errors together. The final list should closely resemble the items circled in the teacher manual.

Lesson Five - Usage and Grammar - Pages 32-39

1. Homework. Ask students to study the usages rules on pages 32-36 and then find the usage errors on page 37. They should not write in their books, but should refer to the errors they find by line number. Go through the errors together. Ask students to tell some usage errors that they did not know were errors.

2. Divide the class into small groups. Each group should study the errors on pages 38-39 and select two from each page that they think are most serious. They must explain why.

Lesson Six - The Grading Process - Pages 40-58

1. Read pages 40-42 aloud together, pausing for comments and questions.

2. For each sample paper, have students read the text and study the paper. Discuss why that paper received the grade that it did, before moving on to the next paper.

3. Read the Key Point Summary on page 58 aloud together. Ask students which point they think is most important and why they think so. Give students a short time to think about the question: What is the most important thing that you have learned? Discuss. Explain to the students what you expect from them, and what you are most emphatic about.

The Assignment Components

The four assignment papers provide a graduated continuum of instruction, with each assignment adding details. The assignments contain sample pages to examine, vocabulary and grammar pages, and special focus areas. These may be followed by additional content such as outline examples. The assignment concludes with the actual specifications of the paper to be written.

The best approach is to spend one period introducing each assignment. Examine the initial sample page. Go over the vocabulary and grammar components, just to put students in an academic writer's frame of mind.

The Vocabulary Page

The vocabulary page always displays ten all-purpose academic words taken from *The Word Within the Word, Volume One*. The point of the page is to reinforce those words and to accustom students to the difference between *formal words* appropriate for academic writing and casual, informal, slang words that do not belong. Read the text aloud and then discuss the questions at the bottom of the page.

Assignment One: Think like an academic writer — about words.

As you write, think carefully about the words you use. You must use words precisely, and you must choose words that have an academic tone. Write with a dictionary close, and never use a word unless you know its definition and part-of-speech usage.

A rule of thumb is that while you want to use only formal vocabulary in your academic writing, and never contractions or clichés (if these occur in quoted material, that is fine), you also do not want to overload your sentences with big words. Good writers typically use only one power-word in a sentence, and do not put them in every sentence. These very strong words are reserved for emphasis, and are often the last word in the sentence because they have more impact there.

One of the ways you learn the tone of academic papers is by absorbing academic vocabulary and getting a feel for how it differs from conversational vocabulary. Here are some formal words from *The Word Within the Word, Volume One*, that are appropriate in a variety of academic papers. Each listing begins with the chapter of *The Word Within the Word* in which it appears:

	Word	Definition	Part of Speech	Example
1.	**superfluous**	excess	adjective	The objection was **superfluous**.
1.	**posthumously**	after death	adverb	The book was published **posthumously**.
2.	**neophyte**	beginner	noun	As a poet, he was a **neophyte**.
2.	**incredulous**	disbelieving	adjective	The readers were **incredulous**.
3.	**specious**	false	adjective	The **specious** argument convinced him.
3.	**elucidate**	explain	verb	Harper Lee **elucidated** the scene.
4.	**equanimity**	calmness	noun	Ahab's **equanimity** was startling.
4.	**magnum opus**	great work	noun	*Walden* was Thoreau's **magnum opus**.
5.	**hyperbole**	overstatement	noun	The claim was mere **hyperbole**.
5.	**altruism**	selflessness	noun	Toad was not known for **altruism**.

The Grammar Page

The grammar page is a thumbnail grammar review, taken from *4Practice, Volume One*. The purpose is to remind students of the elements of the four levels of grammar, but also to display how grammar, vocabulary, poetics, punctuation, and writing techniques work together and interlock in each *sentence*. You might like to review the sentence in the assignment first, and then give them another from *4Practice, Volume One*, to solve.

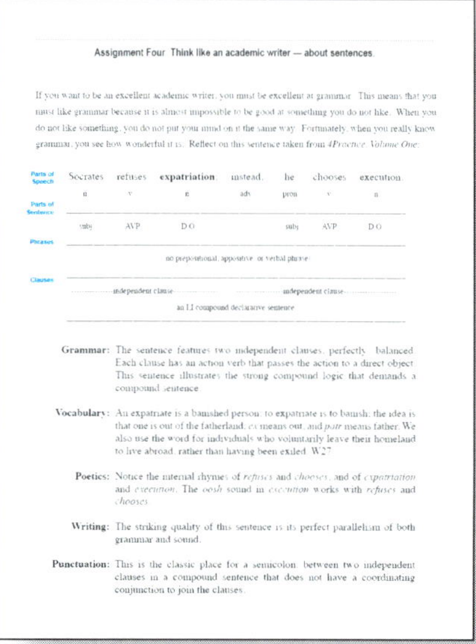

Assignment Four: Think like an academic writer — about sentences.

If you want to be an excellent academic writer, you must be excellent at grammar. This means that you must like grammar because it is almost impossible to be good at something you do not like. When you do not like something, you do not put your mind on it the same way. Fortunately, when you really know grammar, you see how wonderful it is. Reflect on this sentence taken from *4Practice, Volume One*:

Parts of Speech	Socrates	refuses	**expatriation**;	instead,	he	chooses	**execution**.
	n	v	n	adv	pron	v	n
Parts of Sentence	subj	AVP	D.O.		subj	AVP	D.O.
Phrases	no prepositional, appositive, or verbal phrase						
Clauses	independent clause				independent clause		
	an I;I compound declarative sentence						

Grammar: The sentence features two independent clauses, perfectly balanced. Each clause has an action verb that passes the action to a direct object. This sentence illustrates the strong compound logic that demands a compound sentence.

Vocabulary: An expatriate is a banished person; to expatriate is to banish; the idea is that one is out of the fatherland: *ex* means out, and *patr* means father. We also use the word for individuals who voluntarily leave their homeland to live abroad, rather than having been exiled. W27

Poetics: Notice the internal rhymes of *refuses* and *chooses*, and of *expatriation* and *execution*. The *oosh* sound in *execution* works with *refuses* and *chooses*.

Writing: The striking quality of this sentence is its perfect parallelism of both grammar and sound.

Punctuation: This is the classic place for a semicolon: between two independent clauses in a compound sentence that does not have a coordinating conjunction to join the clauses.

Actual Research Paper Comments. Then look carefully at the actual research paper comments. These are exactly as advertised: real, classroom-tested research paper comments saved and refined for years. As I graded stacks of papers each quarter (sometimes each six weeks), I typed out a response *with explanations* of errors to each student (see page 104; more on this later), and rather than retyping, say, the run-on sentence explanation, anew each time, I would save the explanation on my computer. The next time I found a run-on sentence, I had that explanation ready and could easily paste it into my new comment. Over a period of years, my collection of comments grew, and I continually refined and improved them. Eventually I had several hundred comments saved and refined, and I realized that the collection of comments was a real-life database of the most common and serious errors that students make. This database of error explanations, with instructions, is provided for you on CD in the Teacher Manual, so that you can easily copy and paste explanations of errors in your comments to students.

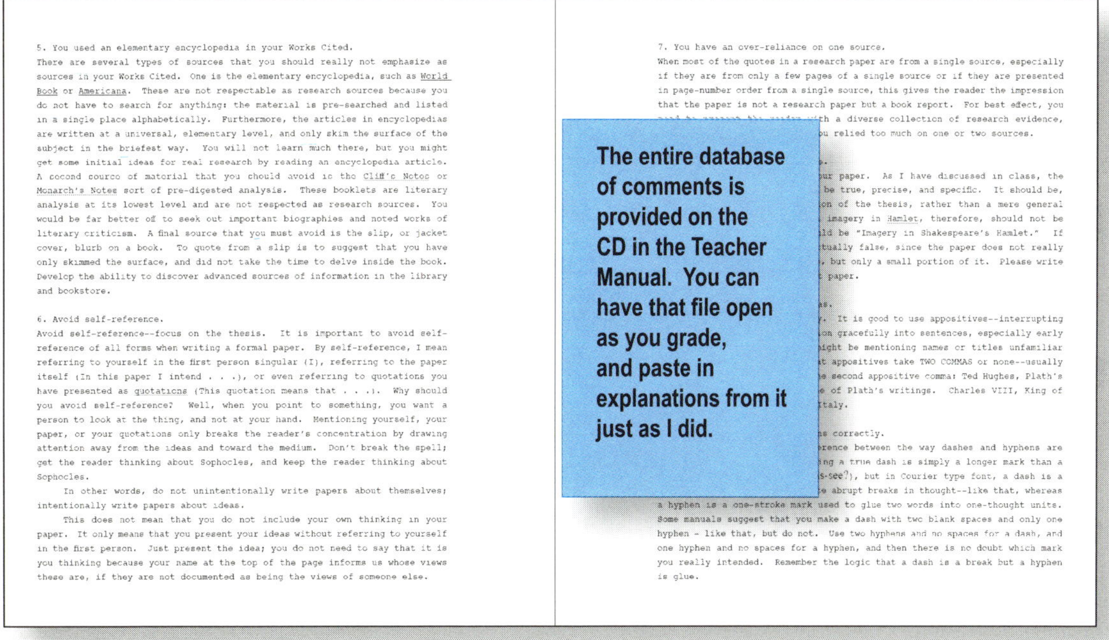

5. You used an elementary encyclopedia in your Works Cited.
There are several types of sources that you should really not emphasize as sources in your Works Cited. One is the elementary encyclopedia, such as World Book or Americana. These are not respectable as research sources because you do not have to search for anything: the material is pre-searched and listed in a single place alphabetically. Furthermore, the articles in encyclopedias are written at a universal, elementary level, and only skim the surface of the subject in the briefest way. You will not learn much there, but you might get some initial ideas for real research by reading an encyclopedia article. A second source of material that you should avoid is the Cliff's Notes or Monarch's Notes sort of pre-digested analysis. These booklets are literary analysis at its lowest level and are not respected as research sources. You would be far better off to seek out important biographies and noted works of literary criticism. A final source that you must avoid is the slip, or jacket cover, blurb on a book. To quote from a slip is to suggest that you have only skimmed the surface, and did not take the time to delve inside the book. Develop the ability to discover advanced sources of information in the library and bookstore.

6. Avoid self-reference.
Avoid self-reference--focus on the thesis. It is important to avoid self-reference of all forms when writing a formal paper. By self-reference, I mean referring to yourself in the first person singular (I), referring to the paper itself (In this paper I intend . . .), or even referring to quotations you have presented as quotations (This quotation means that . . .). Why should you avoid self-reference? Well, when you point to something, you want a person to look at the thing, and not at your hand. Mentioning yourself, your paper, or your quotations only breaks the reader's concentration by drawing attention away from the ideas and toward the medium. Don't break the spell; get the reader thinking about Sophocles, and keep the reader thinking about Sophocles.

In other words, do not unintentionally write papers about themselves; intentionally write papers about ideas.

This does not mean that you do not include your own thinking in your paper. It only means that you present your ideas without referring to yourself in the first person. Just present the idea; you do not need to say that it is you thinking because your name at the top of the page informs us whose views these are, if they are not documented as being the views of someone else.

7. You have an over-reliance on one source.
When most of the quotes in a research paper are from a single source, especially if they are from only a few pages of a single source or if they are presented in page-number order from a single source, this gives the reader the impression that the paper is not a research paper but a book report. For best effect, you

a hyphen is a one-stroke mark used to glue two words into one-thought units. Some manuals suggest that you make a dash with two blank spaces and only one hyphen - like that, but do not. Use two hyphens and no spaces for a dash, and one hyphen and no spaces for a hyphen, and then there is no doubt which mark you really intended. Remember the logic that a dash is a break but a hyphen is glue.

In this book we will focus on forty of these comments, ten per assignment. Ten is enough; one of the mistakes we make in teaching writing is giving students too much too soon. We can afford to pace the program. Some of the comments in the lesson will be new ideas, and others will reinforce details we have already mentioned. These ten comments should be studied intensely, one at a time. Read each one aloud together, and discuss it. Make sure that students understand what is required and why it is important. Make sure they realize that these are standard details that will affect their grade on this and many future papers. Call their attention to the proofreader marks that often accompany the comments. Divide the class into five groups; have each group master two comments and explain them to the class.

Special Content. Following the research paper comments, there are other instructional components; these vary from assignment to assignment. In the first assignment, students can see what a formal outline looks like. In the second assignment there are details about how to do Works Cited listings. Sometimes you will want to examine these passages together; other times you may wish to assign them as homework readings, with a follow-up question or two the next day. Much of this special content serves as reference detail that students can keep referring back to as they write; the key is that they understand it and know where to find it.

The special content in the first assignment concerns outlining, and it will require you to make a judgment call. In my own class I did not require a formal outline. The emphasis on short papers makes the outline seem like overkill. If you want to ask students to do an outline for the first paper, that might be all right, but we do not want the outlining method itself to become an additional learning project that distracts students. For these short papers, we can use the essay structure as its own three-part outline; if students know what they are going to do in the introduction, body, and conclusion, then their essay structure is inherently an outline.

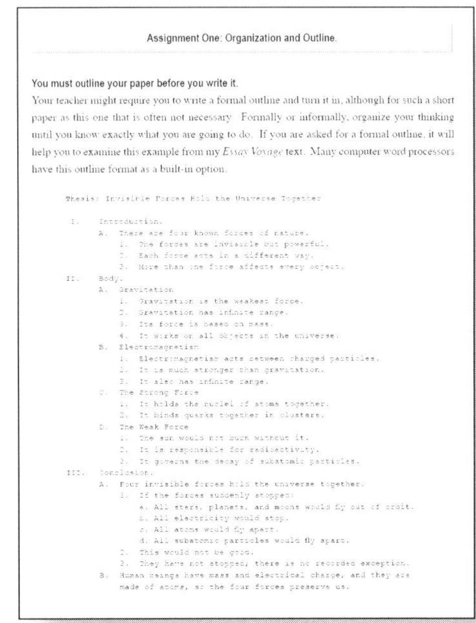
Assignment One: Organization and Outline.

You must outline your paper before you write it.

Your teacher might require you to write a formal outline and turn it in, although for such a short paper as this one that is often not necessary. Formally or informally, organize your thinking until you know exactly what you are going to do. If you are asked for a formal outline, it will help you to examine this example from my *Essay Voyage* text. Many computer word processors have this outline format as a built-in option.

```
Thesis: Invisible Forces Hold the Universe Together

 I.   Introduction.
      A.  There are four known forces of nature.
          1.  The forces are invisible but powerful.
          2.  Each force acts in a different way.
          3.  More than one force affects every object.
 II.  Body.
      A.  Gravitation
          1.  Gravitation is the weakest force.
          2.  Gravitation has infinite range.
          3.  Its force is based on mass.
          4.  It works on all objects in the universe.
      B.  Electromagnetism
          1.  Electromagnetism acts between charged particles.
          2.  It is much stronger than gravitation.
          3.  It also has infinite range.
      C.  The Strong Force
          1.  It holds the nuclei of atoms together.
          2.  It binds quarks together in clusters.
      D.  The Weak Force
          1.  The sun would not burn without it.
          2.  It is responsible for radioactivity.
          3.  It governs the decay of subatomic particles.
 III. Conclusion.
      A.  Four invisible forces hold the universe together.
          1.  If the forces suddenly stopped:
              a. All stars, planets, and moons would fly out of orbit.
              b. All electricity would stop.
              c. All atoms would fly apart.
              d. All subatomic particles would fly apart.
          2.  This would not be good.
          3.  They have not stopped; there is no recorded exception.
      B.  Human beings have mass and electrical charge, and they are
          made of atoms, so the four forces preserve us.
```

The Assignment Specifications. At the end of each assignment are the specifications for the paper. These include purpose, topic, length, due date, format, structure, source information, and a reminder about the honor pledge. There are often sample pages for students to look at because students need to *see* what these elements look like; a core strategy of this book is to *show* students, over and over (and over), what good papers (and bad ones) look like.

Some specifications are variable and flexible; you should create an optimum fit for your own classroom. You may wish to nudge the topic closer to your curriculum focus. You will need to schedule the due date, and schedule an appropriate amount of library time. Although I used this method with success for many years, I do not regard the details as dogma; you should change any detail rather than force a square peg into a round curriculum. In this book I try to point a true path as you and I work together.

The Grading Method

I have discussed some aspects of my grading method to the students in the student book, but there are professional aspects of the implementation that we need to discuss. I know that each of us is a different person in a different situation, and that you will need to modify the grading method as you see best, but I will show you the method that gave me the best results in student learning. In grading academic writing, the student outcome reflects the quality of the teacher input.

My grading method evolved during a period of many years, as I tried and rejected others that did not feel writerly and did not produce enough change in student writing. I felt responsible for preparing the students to do the academic writing that would let them excel in all of their courses. I did not want to give students merely some exposure to academic writing; I wanted to move them dramatically forward in their ability to write. If actual success is the goal, then there are inexorable implications, including multiple papers and an extraordinarily professional approach to grading.

A Mutual Commitment. Any program that proposes to change students from being unable to write academically to being able to do it will require a powerful commitment from students and teachers alike. To write high-level papers in each term is a major proposition; it will involve a significant fraction of the available class time, it will occupy a great deal of independent work and homework from students, it will commit the teacher to long hours of grading at night and on weekends, and it will require the support of the administration and parents. Such a program is a choice that demands the necessary resources of time and energy if it is to succeed. I have no doubt that the outcome is so crucial to students' futures that it easily justifies such extraordinary commitment. The more that all groups—students, teachers, administrators, and parents—are on board, the greater success students will have.

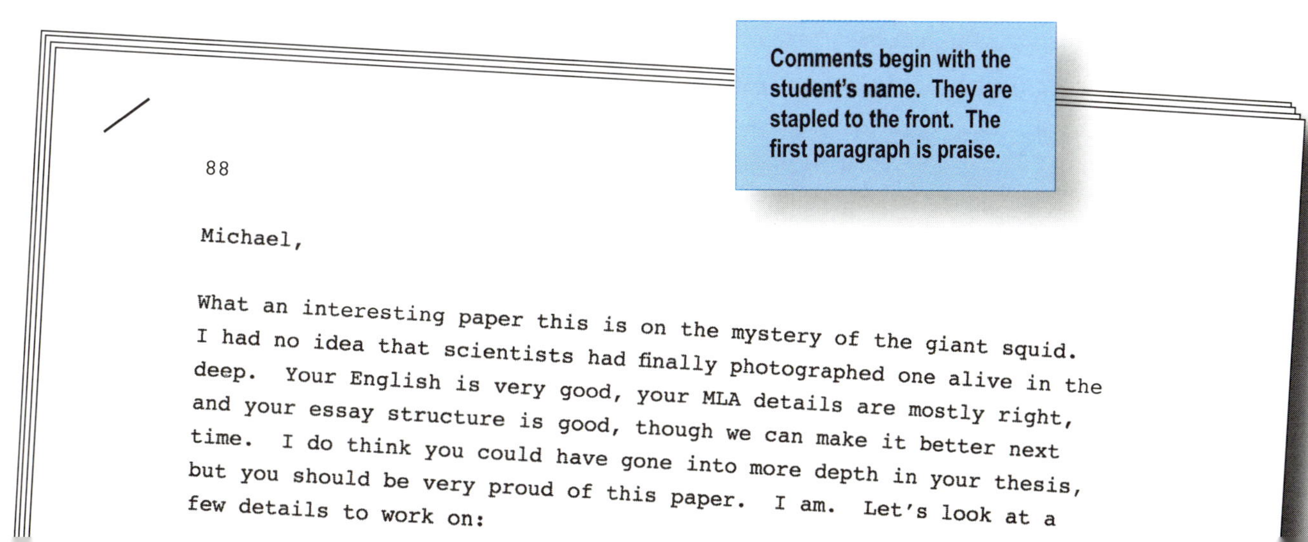

Comprehensive Grammar Preparation. On an advanced academic paper, student grammar must be graded, so the truth is that teaching academic writing and grading academic writing require the teacher to have a strong knowledge of grammar. Grammar is the foundation for correct academic sentences. Absent grammar, there is no competent way to know whether sentences are correct or not; the "ear" hears social grammar. Both teachers and students must arrive at this book with a strong grammar foundation. *The Magic Lens* provides a front-loaded, compacted grammar instruction that can be done at the beginning of the year.

Writing and Grading Employ the Same Standards. It is best to avoid a discrepancy between the writing standards enforced upon the students and the grading standards employed by the teacher. We all remember the disappointment we felt when a paper was returned to us with inadequate, unexplained, or semi-comprehensible marks and comments scrawled on the paper—or worse, when we received a paper that had a grade without explanation. If we ask students to type their papers and use standard English, then we should write or type our comments in standard English. We have reached a point where computers with word processors are ubiquitous, in schools and in homes, and virtually every student and teacher can prepare a professional document. The grading process can be literary and academic. The more professional we make our evaluation, the more respect students will have for it, and the more they will appreciate the commitment we have made to them.

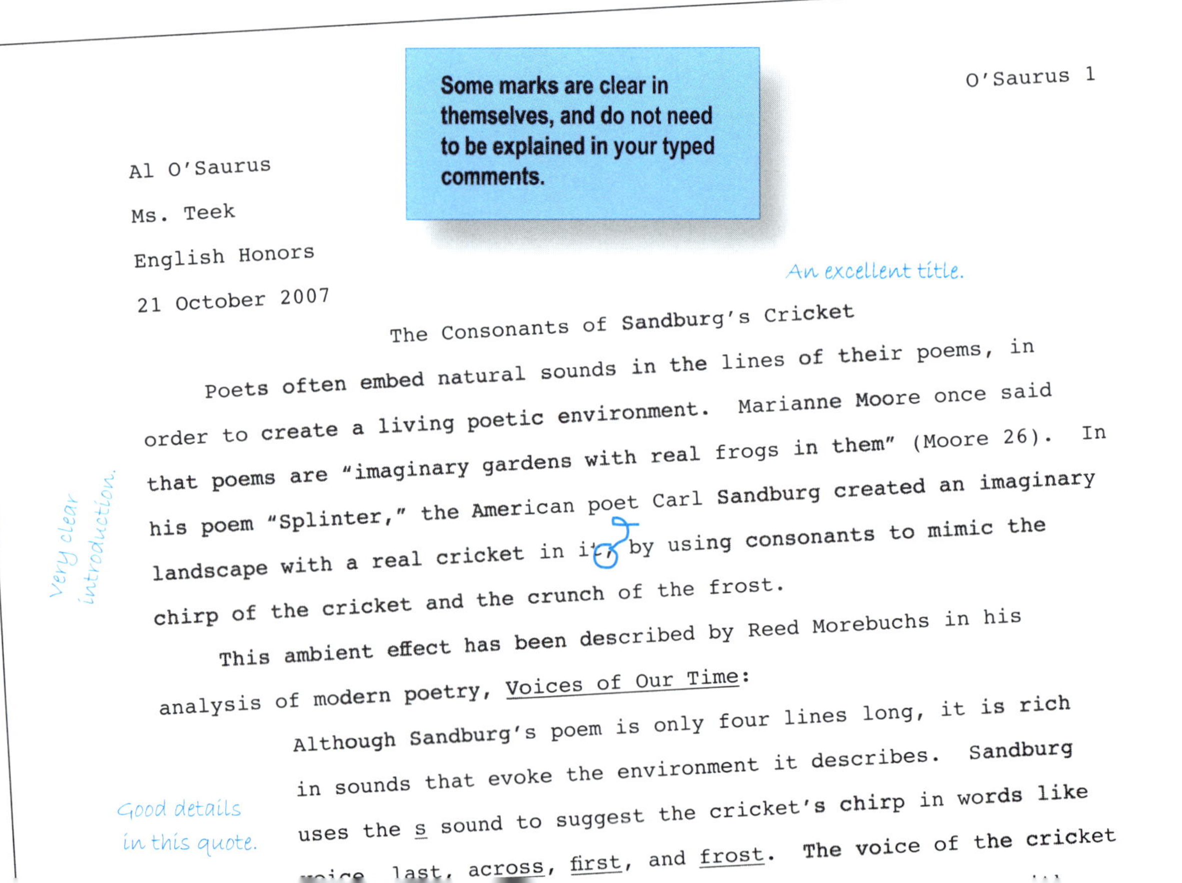

Some marks are clear in themselves, and do not need to be explained in your typed comments.

O'Saurus 1

Al O'Saurus

Ms. Teek

English Honors

21 October 2007

An excellent title.

The Consonants of Sandburg's Cricket

Poets often embed natural sounds in the lines of their poems, in order to create a living poetic environment. Marianne Moore once said that poems are "imaginary gardens with real frogs in them" (Moore 26). In his poem "Splinter," the American poet Carl Sandburg created an imaginary landscape with a real cricket in it, by using consonants to mimic the chirp of the cricket and the crunch of the frost.

Very clear introduction.

This ambient effect has been described by Reed Morebuchs in his analysis of modern poetry, <u>Voices of Our Time</u>:

> Although Sandburg's poem is only four lines long, it is rich in sounds that evoke the environment it describes. Sandburg uses the <u>s</u> sound to suggest the cricket's chirp in words like voice, last, <u>across</u>, <u>first</u>, and <u>frost</u>. The voice of the cricket

Good details in this quote.

Recommendations: from Assigning to Collecting Papers

1. Have students study the components of the assignment as described earlier. Inform students of any modifications you wish to make in order to integrate the topic with your curriculum. Give students the library time they need (most likely at least two or more class periods, depending upon the assignment). Give them two weeks or more to write their papers.

2. Shortly before the paper is due, discuss again what real proofreading is. Remind students that they should look up every detail of grammar, punctuation, or spelling, and that they cannot pass if the paper is filled with basic errors. Offer to answer any questions before the due date. Remind them that only MLA papers will be accepted, and that the penalty for late papers is one letter grade per day. Remind them that they must write the honor pledge, and that any plagiarism will result in a grade of zero.

3. On the due date, collect the papers. Be sure that every paper has the honor pledge. If a paper is not in MLA format, do not accept it. Return it to the student to be redone as assigned.

Grading Papers

1. When you grade a paper, sit at the computer. Open a new word processing document before you begin to read, and type the student's name. Also open the comments file provided on the CD in the teacher manual; with both documents open, you can easily transfer comments.

2. As you read the paper, use a pen, not pencil, to put marks, abbreviations, and brief comments on the student's paper. Praise good details. Correct mistakes, as much as possible, with the standard proofreading marks provided in this book. Be specific; rather than saying *Good!*, say *Good transition*. Use words; do not put numbers or point deductions on the paper.

98

Al,

What an insightful paper this is on the poetic technique in Carl Sandburg's "Splinter." You obviously have thought carefully and read closely, and your paper is very perceptive. Your technical details are advanced; the English is excellent, the MLA format is perfect, and the essay structure is clear and connected. I am very proud of what you have accomplished. Let's look at a few details:

Page 1: Your introduction is outstanding. It is succinct and interesting, and the Moore quote you include is perfect

3. The grading should be informative. As you discover problems in the student's paper, explain them. Pause and type a short explanation in the word-processing document. Use Courier, just like the student papers, but rather than double-space use space-and-a-half or single-space, whichever you prefer. The typed comments should be in complete sentences and should exactly follow the writing standards asked of the students. For this step, you will not have to compose every comment yourself, because you now have access to the CD collection of explanations that you can easily copy and paste into your comments.

It is important to be positive when a student has done something well, but it is even more important to be positive when they have not. The tone we must take with mistakes is explanatory and helpful. We correct problems with a calm, professional encouragement. The more problems the paper has, the more important it is to be positive and show the student that we really believe in him or her, and that the next papers will be much better, with their hard work and our help. We do not want a single student to feel crushed and that he or she can never learn to do this.

After you finish correcting the paper, including marking on the paper itself and typing or pasting the explanations, go back to the beginning of your comment page, put a grade above the student's name, type a positive first paragraph below the student's name, and also make sure that there is a positive conclusion at the end. Print the comment and staple it to the student's paper.

The grading method is explained earlier, but here let us note that it is not arrived at through numerical addition or subtraction. Instead, there are points of accomplishment that students must reach: good English for a D, MLA too for a C, essay structure too for a B, and an idea for an A. We must be reasonable; even the best students will make a few basic English mistakes. Once a student is eligible for a certain grade, but not the grade above it, then we adjust the points within that grade up or down to account for overall accomplishments or problems. A student cannot jump levels; a student who has good English but bad MLA format cannot get a B, even if he or she has good essay structure.

Returning the Papers

Make every effort to return papers promptly. If possible, return them within a week. Before passing the papers out, remind the students that they are supposed to be learners; if they already knew all of this, there would be no reason for the assignment. Tell them that regardless of the grade on this paper, each one of them has the ability to write wonderful papers this year, and that together we will make it happen.

98

Al,

What an insightful paper this is on the poetic technique in Carl Sandburg's "Splinter." You obviously have thought carefully and read closely, and your paper is very perceptive. Your technical details are advanced; the English is excellent, the MLA format is perfect, and the essay structure is clear and connected. I am very proud of what you have accomplished. Let's look at a few details:

You have done a good job punctuating the clauses in your sentences. I do not see any run-on sentences or comma splices in the paper. Attention to details like that makes a big difference in how pleasant a paper is for a reader to read.

Page 1: Your introduction is outstanding. It is succinct and interesting, and the Moore quote you include is perfect.

Page 2: You have D,I clause punctuation error. Remember that when you have a complex sentence beginning with a dependent clause, you are required to put a comma after the introductory dependent clause.

Page 3: Avoid exaggeration. Beware of exaggerated claims and unsupported generalities. If you claim that "no other author has ever" done something, what is your evidence? Are you prepared to discuss the work of every other author and demonstrate its inadequacy? The "most people" error also falls in this category. If you claim that most people think x, do you have evidence in the form of polls or statistics or even quotations from social science that a majority of people think x, or are you just exaggerating? In a formal paper you do not guess or exaggerate; your statements are expected to be the truth; accurate and defensible just as they are expressed.

Page 3: I love your witty comment that Sandburg was a micro-poet!

Again, I am very impressed with your paper. Thank you for doing such a great job. Keep concentrating on the basics of English and on the quality of your ideas, as you have here. I will look forward to your next paper.

Overview and Key Points

Volume One of *Advanced Academic Writing* is devoted to the four basic elements of advanced academic writing (good English, correct format, essay form, and a worthwhile topic) that will lead students to success in their academic classes, whether middle school, high school, or college. The emphasis in this first book is on the *intensity* of learning, rather than on the number of details; what students must realize, from the very beginning, is how serious academic standards are.

Like my vocabulary, grammar, and poetics programs, which provide important foundations for advanced academic writing, this program assumes that motivated students are capable of much more than they are sometimes asked to do, and that the curricular grade level limitations prevalent in the country do more to hinder education than to promote it. When it comes to serious education, we have to have high goals and high assumptions about student ability.

The program makes demands not only on students; it makes demands on teachers too. It is not a program for teachers who want to make writing instruction easier; rather, this is a program for confident teachers who know they are professionals, and who want high-level assignments and grading methods that they are proud to implement.

The heart of the method is to align writing instruction with the standards students will actually face in their future academic lives, and then to align the instruction and grading with the deep human spirit of writing. I have rejected over-meticulous point systems that reduce grading to a series of nervous subtractions from 100, and have presented a grading logic that expresses the logic of writing itself. The grading method is therefore not a something-else, a separate thing, a distraction, a corruption of the concentration of the writer; rather, to get the grade the student has to think like a writer.

The final goal is that when students finish this first program, they have a new, calm confidence about advanced academic writing, and that they feel extremely fortunate to have been in your class.

Three Punctuation Quizzes

Because every sentence must be punctuated, punctuation is a critical skill. Academic punctuation is a function of grammar, so it is worth a significant investment of time to make sure that students understand how and why to punctuate.

The recommendation for these quizzes: let students work on them in small groups, open book, then discuss the answers afterwards.

You can copy the quiz and distribute it to the students.

Punctuation as a Function of Grammar: Quiz One

For each of the following sentences, circle the letter of each answer that is true. The answer can be any combination, including all or none. This exercise will teach you the real process of punctuation as a function of grammar.

1. At the beginning of the poem the scoundrel wrote Bring me some beans.

a. a comma after the prepositional phrases
b. an apostrophe in the contraction
c. a comma before the direct quotation
d. quotation marks around the direct quotation
e. a period inside the closing quotation marks

2. When Stevenson wrote Treasure Island he created an unforgettable story.

a. a comma after the independent clause
b. an apostrophe in the possessive noun
c. a comma after the dependent clause
d. italics on the novel title
e. quotation marks around the novel title

3. A two thirds majority of the students wanted pencils paper and snacks.

a. a hyphen in the compound adjective
b. a colon at the beginning of the list
c. a comma after the plural common noun
d. a list comma before the coordinating conjunction
e. a comma after the dependent clause

4. Climbing rapidly upward the exhausted bear found its cave.

a. a comma after the prepositional phrase
b. comma between adj.'s preceding the noun
c. a comma after the participial phrase
d. a comma after the gerund phrase
e. an apostrophe in the contraction

5. Libro is the Spanish word for book it is a good word to know.

a. quotation marks around the Spanish noun
b. italics on the Spanish noun
c. a comma after the independent clause
d. a comma after the dependent clause
e. a semicolon after the independent clause

Punctuation as a Function of Grammar: Quiz One

1. At the beginning of the poem, the scoundrel wrote, "Bring me some beans."

a. a comma after the prepositional phrases

b. an apostrophe in the contraction

c. a comma before the direct quotation

d. quotation marks around the direct quotation

e. a period inside the closing quotation marks

A comma after multiple introductory prepositional phrases. The American standard is to put the period inside the closing quotes, although corporations and the British often put it outside.

2. When Stevenson wrote *Treasure Island,* he created an unforgettable story.

a. a comma after the independent clause

b. an apostrophe in the possessive noun

c. a comma after the dependent clause

d. italics on the novel title

e. quotation marks around the novel title

We need a D,I comma after the introductory dependent clause in this complex sentence, and titles of novels are al ways in italics.

3. A two-thirds majority of the students wanted pencils, paper, and snacks.

a. a hyphen in the compound adj.

b. a colon at the beginning of the list

c. a comma after the plural common noun

d. a list comma before the coordinating conj.

e. a comma after the dependent clause

A hyphen makes *two-thirds* a compound adjective. We prefer to put the list comma before the coordinating conjunction, though some style manuals do not require it.

4. Climbing rapidly upward, the exhausted bear found its cave.

a. a comma after the prepositional phrase

b. comma between adjectives preceding the noun

c. a comma after the participial phrase

d. a comma after the gerund phrase

e. an apostrophe in the contraction

5. *Libro* is the Spanish word for book; it is a good word to know.

a. quotation marks around the Spanish noun

b. italics on the Spanish noun

c. a comma after the independent clause

d. a comma after the dependent clause

e. a semicolon after the independent clause

When we refer to a word as such or to a foreign-language word, we should always put it in italics. We also put a semicolon between the two clauses of a compound sentence if there isn't a coordinating conjunction joining them.

Punctuation as a Function of Grammar: Quiz Two

For each of the following sentences, circle the letter of each answer that is true. The answer can be any combination, including all or none. This exercise will teach you the real process of punctuation as a function of grammar.

1. In June the publisher lost its most important writer when Shakespeare resigned.

a. a comma after the prepositional phrase
b. a comma after the month
c. an apostrophe in the possessive pronoun
d. an apostrophe in the contraction
e. a comma between the clauses

2. While Dickens was writing we looked over his shoulder.

a. a comma after the participial phrase
b. a comma after the dependent clause
c. a comma after the independent clause
d. a semicolon between the clauses
e. a comma after the prepositional phrase

3. The well intentioned poet wrote two poems today one yesterday and one then.

a. a hyphen in the compound adjective
b. a colon before the list
c. a comma after *today*
d. a list comma after *yesterday*
e. a comma between the clauses

4. Sailing during the weekend was the seamans first plan.

a. a comma after the introductory participial phrase
b. a comma after the dependent clause
c. an apostrophe in the possessive noun
d. commas around the appositive phrase
e. commas around the parenthetical remark

5. Ugh the students found twenty two errors in first three pages.

a. a comma after the introductory adverb
b. a comma after the interjection
c. a comma after the dependent clause
d. a hyphen in the compound adjective
e. a comma before the prepositional phrase

Punctuation as a Function of Grammar: Quiz Two

1. In June the publisher lost its most important writer when Shakespeare resigned.

a. a comma after the prepositional phrase

b. a comma after the month

c. an apostrophe in the possessive pronoun

d. an apostrophe in the contraction

e. a comma between the clauses

No punctuation needed; this is a complex sentence with an ID clause structure.

2. While Dickens was writing, we looked over his shoulder.

a. a comma after the participial phrase

b. a comma after the dependent clause

c. a comma after the independent clause

d. a semicolon between the clauses

e. a comma after the prepositional phrase

This is a D,I complex sentence that begins with a subordinating conjunction to introduce the dependent clause.

3. The well-intentioned poet wrote two poems today, one yesterday, and one then.

a. a hyphen in the compound adjective

b. a colon before the list

c. a comma after *today*

d. a list comma after yesterday

e. a comma between the clauses

Again, though some style manuals will now abandon the list comma before the coordinating conjunction, we feel it best to retain it.

4. Sailing during the weekend was the seaman's first plan.

a. a comma after the introductory participial phrase

b. a comma after the dependent clause

c. an apostrophe in the possessive noun

d. commas around the appositive phrase

e. commas around the parenthetical remark

We will not put a comma after the gerund phrase because it is the subject of the sentence.

5. Ugh, the students found twenty-two errors in the first three pages.

a. a comma after the introductory adverb

b. a comma after the interjection

c. a comma after the dependent clause

d. a hyphen in the compound adjective

e. a comma before the prepositional phrase

An interjection has no grammatical function, so it should be separated with a comma.

Punctuation as a Function of Grammar: Quiz Three

For each of the following sentences, circle the letter of each answer that is true. The answer can be any combination, including all or none. This exercise will teach you the real process of punctuation as a function of grammar.

1. Among the most dedicated readers a reason for reading is not required.

a. comma after introductory prepositional phrase
b. a comma after the dependent clause
c. commas around the parenthetical remark
d. a semicolon between the independent clauses
e. a hyphen in the compound adjective

2. The novelists who wrote the suspenseful mysteries were already known for their talent.

a. commas around the appositive
b. a semicolon between the independent clauses
c. commas around the nonessential clause
d. quotation marks around the word *mysteries*
e. a comma before the infinitive

3. Ben Jonson the Poet Laureate was reluctant however its expected that he will attend.

a. commas around the appositive
b. a semicolon between the independent clauses
c. a comma after *however*
d. an apostrophe in the contraction
e. a comma after the dependent clause

4. In the chilling storm of 34 the scribe scribbled cs and ds in Dickens journal.

a. an apostrophe before the contraction
b. comma after the introductory prep. phrases
c. an apostrophe and s in the possessive noun
d. italics on the letter as such
e. apostrophe in the plural letter as such

5. The shy and rarely seen composer was recently seen at her mailbox.

a. comma between adjectives preceding the subject
b. a comma after the independent clause
c. a semicolon between the independent clauses
d. a comma before the prepositional phrases
e. a comma before the participial phrase

Punctuation as a Function of Grammar: Quiz Three

1. Among the most dedicated readers, a reason for reading is not required.

a. comma after introductory prepositional phrase

b. a comma after the dependent clause

c. commas around the parenthetical remark

d. a semicolon between the independent clauses

e. a hyphen in the compound adjective

This introductory prepositional phrase is long enough to merit a comma.

2. The novelists who wrote the suspenseful mysteries were already known for their talent.

a. commas around the appositive

b. a semicolon between the independent clauses

c. commas around the nonessential clause

d. quotation marks around the word *mysteries*

e. a comma before the infinitive

This sentence contains an adjective clause modifying the subject, but the question is, is the adjective clause essential or nonessential? The best answer is that the clause is essential. Therefore, we do not need to enclose it in commas because it needs to be there.

3. Ben Jonson, the Poet Laureate, was reluctant; however, it's expected that he will attend.

a. commas around the appositive

b. a semicolon between the independent clauses

c. a comma after *however*

d. an apostrophe in the contraction

e. a comma after the dependent clause

This shows the correct treatment of a compound sentence in which the second clause begins with the word *however*.

4. In the chilling storm of '34, the scribe scribbled *c*'s and *d*'s in Dickens's journal.

a. an apostrophe before the contraction

b. comma after the introductory prep. phrases

c. an apostrophe and s in the possessive noun

d. italics on the letter as such

e. apostrophe in the plural letter as such

Lots of punctuation here. Remember that letters, numbers, and words as such are always in italics (or underlined). If you mean the word dog, rather than the four-footed kind, you italicize dog.

5. The shy and rarely seen composer was recently seen at her mailbox.

a. comma between adjectives preceding the subject

b. a comma after the independent clause

c. a semicolon between the independent clauses

d. a comma before the prepositional phrases

e. a comma before the participial phrase

No punctuation.